みんなの日本語

初級I 第2版

Minna no Nihongo

Elementary Japanese I
Translation & Grammar Notes—English

翻訳・文法解説
英語版

スリーエーネットワーク

Published by 3A Corporation.
Trusty Kojimachi Bldg., 2F, 4, Kojimachi 3-Chome, Chiyoda-ku, Tokyo 102-0083, Japan

ISBN978-4-88319-604-3 C0081

First published 1998
Second Edition 2012
Printed in Japan

FOREWORD

As the title *Minna no Nihongo* indicates, this book has been designed to make the study of Japanese as enjoyable and interesting as possible for students and teachers alike. Over three years in the planning and compilation, it stands as a complete textbook in itself while acting as a companion volume to the highly-regarded *Shin Nihongo no Kiso*.

As readers may know, *Shin Nihongo no Kiso* is a comprehensive introduction to elementary Japanese that serves as a highly efficient resource enabling students wishing to master basic Japanese conversation to do so in the shortest possible time. As such, although it was originally developed for use by AOTS's technical trainees, it is now used by a wide range of people both in Japan and abroad.

The teaching of Japanese is branching out in many different ways. Japanese economic and industrial growth has led to a greater level of interchange between Japan and other countries, and non-Japanese from a wide variety of backgrounds have come to Japan with a range of different objectives and are now living within local communities here. The changes in the social milieu surrounding the teaching of Japanese that have resulted from this influx of people from other countries have in turn influenced the individual situations in which Japanese is taught. There is now a greater diversity of learning needs, and they require individual responses.

It is against this background, and in response to the opinions and hopes expressed by a large number of people who have been involved in the teaching of Japanese for many years both in Japan and elsewhere, that 3A Corporation proudly publishes *Minna no Nihongo*. While the book continues to make use of the clarity and ease of understanding provided by the special features, key learning points and learning methods of *Shin Nihongo no Kiso*, the scenes, situations and characters in *Minna no Nihongo* have been made more universal in order to appeal to a wider range of learners. Its contents have been enhanced in this way to allow all kinds of students to use it for studying Japanese with pleasure.

Minna no Nihongo is aimed at anyone who urgently needs to learn to communicate in Japanese in any situation, whether at work, school, college or in their local community. Although it is an introductory text, efforts have been made to make the exchanges between Japanese and foreign characters in the book reflect Japanese social conditions and everyday life as faithfully as possible. While it is intended principally for those who have already left full-time education, it can also be recommended as an excellent textbook for university entrance courses as well as for short-term intensive courses at technical colleges and universities.

We at 3A Corporation are continuing actively to produce new study materials designed to meet the individual needs of an increasingly wide range of learners, and we sincerely hope that readers will continue to give us their valued support.

In conclusion, I should like to mention the extensive help we received in the preparation of this text, in the form of suggestions and comments from various quarters, and trials of the materials in actual lessons, for which we are extremely grateful. 3A Corporation intends to continue extending its network of friendship all over the world through activities such as the publishing of Japanese study materials, and we hope that everyone who knows us will continue to lend us their unstinting encouragement and support in this.

Iwao Ogawa
President, 3A Corporation
March 1998

FOREWORD TO THE SECOND EDITION
— On the Publication of the Second Edition of *Minna no Nihongo Shokyu* —

We are proud to publish the second edition of *Minna no Nihongo Shokyu*. As stated in the Foreword to the first edition, *Minna no Nihongo Shokyu* can be regarded as a companion volume to *Shin Nihongo no Kiso*, a textbook originally developed for technical trainees.

The first printing of the first edition of *Minna no Nihongo Shokyu I* was issued in March 1998, when great changes in the social environment surrounding the teaching of Japanese were taking place. The burgeoning of relationships between Japan and the rest of the world had led to a rapid increase in the number of students of Japanese and their reasons for studying the language, and the consequent diversification of their requirements had necessitated a response more tailored to learners' individual situations. 3A Corporation published *Minna no Nihongo Shokyu* in response to suggestions and comments received from people on the front lines of Japanese teaching in Japan and elsewhere.

Minna no Nihongo Shokyu was acclaimed for its easily-understood key learning points and methods, its high degree of general applicability that took into account learners' diversity, and for being a carefully-crafted learning resource that was outstandingly effective for students attempting to master Japanese conversation quickly. It has served well for over ten years, but any language changes with the times, and both Japan and other countries have experienced great upheavals recently. Particularly in the last few years, the environment in which the Japanese language and its learners are situated has changed drastically.

In these circumstances, 3A Corporation decided to review and partially revise *Minna no Nihongo Shokyu I* and *II*, based on our publishing and training experience and reflecting the many opinions and questions we have received from students and teachers of Japanese, in order to be able to contribute further to the teaching of Japanese as a foreign language.

The revision focused on making the book even more usable and changing any words or scenarios that no longer reflected current conditions. Respecting the wishes of students and teachers, we have preserved the original textbook format, which has the benefit of making the book easy to use for both learning and teaching, and we have introduced more exercises and practice questions designed to strengthen students' active language ability by inviting them to understand situations for themselves and think about how to express themselves, rather than merely following instructions and practising in a passive way. We have included a large number of illustrations for this purpose.

We are extremely grateful for the enormous help we received in the editing of this book, in the form of comments and suggestions from various quarters, and trials in actual lessons. 3A Corporation intends to continue developing textbooks that can not only help students of Japanese to communicate what they need to but also contribute to international interpersonal interchange, and we hope that everyone engaged in such activities will find them useful. We warmly invite everyone who knows us to continue to lend us their unstinting encouragement and support in this.

Takuji Kobayashi
President, 3A Corporation
June 2012

TO USERS OF THIS BOOK

I. Structure

The second edition of ***Minna no Nihongo Shokyu I*** consists of two volumes: the Main Text (with CD) and the Translation and Grammar Notes. We plan to publish the Translation and Grammar Notes in twelve languages, starting with English.

The materials have been compiled with the aim of inculcating the four skills of speaking, listening, reading and writing. However the Main Text and the Translation and Grammar Notes do not provide any instruction in reading and writing hiragana, katakana, or kanji.

II. Contents

1. Main Text

1) Japanese Pronunciation

This section gives examples of the chief points to note concerning Japanese pronunciation.

2) Classroom Language, Everyday Greetings and Expressions, Numerals

This section contains a list of words and phrases used in the classroom, basic everyday greetings, and so on.

3) Lessons

There are 25 lessons, each containing the following:

① Sentence patterns

Basic sentence patterns to be learned in that lesson.

② Example sentences

Basic sentence patterns incorporated into short dialogues to show how they are used in actual conversation. New adverbs, conjunctions, and other parts of speech, plus further learning points, are also introduced.

③ Conversation

In the conversation, foreign people living in Japan appear in a variety of situations. The conversation includes everyday greetings and other expressions and as well as the material to be learned in the lesson. If time allows, students can try developing the conversation by introducing some of the Useful Words given in the Translation and Grammar Notes.

④ Exercises

The exercises are split into three levels: A, B, and C.
Exercise A is laid out visually to help students understand the grammatical structure easily. It has been designed to make it easy for students to practise

conjugating verbs and forming connections, as well as mastering the basic sentence patterns.

Exercise B employs various forms to strengthen students' grasp of the basic sentence patterns. A number with an arrow (➡) indicates an exercise that uses an illustration.

Exercise C is designed to help students improve their communication abilities. Students use this exercise to practise conversing while substituting the underlined words in the designated conversation with alternatives matching the situation; however, to prevent this becoming a simple substitution drill, we have wherever possible avoided using words to indicate substitutions. This means that the exercises are very free, with students able to create various different conversational examples based on a single illustration.

Model answers to Exercises B and C are available in a separate compilation volume.

⑤ Practice questions

There are three types of practice question: listening comprehension, grammar, and reading comprehension. The listening comprehension questions are further subdivided into two types: answering short questions, and listening to short conversations and grasping the key points. The grammar questions check students' understanding of vocabulary and grammar points. For the reading comprehension questions, students read a simple passage incorporating vocabulary and grammar they have already studied, and perform various types of task relating to its contents.

⑥ Review

This is provided to enable students to go over the essential points once more every few lessons.

⑦ Summary of Adverbs, Conjunctions and Conversational Expressions

These are practice questions designed to enable students to review the adverbs, conjunctions and conversational expressions presented in this textbook.

4) Verb forms

This section summarises the verb forms presented in this textbook, together with various forms added to the ends of verbs.

5) Table of Key Learning Points

This is a summary of the key learning points presented in this textbook, focusing on Exercise A. It indicates which of the Sentence Patterns, Example Sentences, and Exercises B and C are relevant to each of the learning points introduced in Exercise A.

6) Index

This includes Classroom Language, Everyday Greetings and Expressions, and new vocabulary and expressions appearing in each lesson, with references to the lesson in which they first appear.

7) Included CD

The CD that goes with this book contains the conversation and the listening comprehension exercises from each lesson.

2. Translation and Grammar notes

1) Explanations of the general features of Japanese, as well as the Japanese writing and pronunciation systems.

2) Translations of Classroom Language, and Everyday Greetings and Expressions.

3) The following for each of Lessons 1 through 25:

① New words and their translations.

② Translations of Sentence Patterns, Example Sentences and Conversations.

③ Useful words relevant to each lesson and snippets of information on Japan.

④ Explanations of the grammar of the Sentence Patterns and expressions.

4) A summary of how to express numbers, time, and time periods, a list of counter suffixes, and conjugations of verbs.

III. Time Required to Complete the Lessons

As a guideline, it should take students 4-6 hours to cover each lesson, and 150 hours to finish the entire book.

IV. Vocabulary

The book presents approximately 1,000 words, mainly ones used frequently in daily life.

V. Kanji Usage

Wherever possible, kanji used in this book have been selected from the list of Kanji for Regular Use (Joyo Kanji) announced by the Japanese Cabinet in 1981.

1) 熟字訓 (words that are formed from two or more kanji and have a special reading) which appear in the Appendix to the Joyo Kanji list are written in kanji:

e.g. 友達 friend　果物 fruit　眼鏡 spectacles

2) Some kanji and readings not appearing in the Joyo Kanji list have been used in place names, people's names and other proper nouns, and in words from artistic, cultural and other specialised fields:

e.g. 大阪 Osaka　奈良 Nara　歌舞伎 kabuki

3) To make the text easier to read, some words have been written in kana even though they appear in the Joyo Kanji list:

e.g. ある(有る・在る)　have・exist　　たぶん(多分)　probably
きのう(昨日)　yesterday

4) Numbers are usually shown as Arabic numerals:

e.g. 9時　nine o'clock　　4月1日　1st April　　1つ　one

VI. Miscellaneous

1) Words that can be omitted are enclosed in square brackets:

e.g. 父は 54[歳]です。　My father is 54 [years old].

2) Synonymous words and expressions are enclosed in round brackets:

e.g. だれ(どなた)　who

HOW TO USE THIS BOOK EFFECTIVELY

1. Learn the words

The Translation and Grammar Notes introduces the new words for each lesson. Learn these new words by practising making short sentences with them.

2. Practise the Sentence Patterns

Make sure you understand the meaning of each sentence pattern, and do Exercises A and B aloud until the pattern becomes automatic.

3. Practise holding conversations

Practise the sentence patterns using the short dialogues given in Exercise C, but don't stop there; carry on and extend the conversations. The conversations simulate everyday situations that students are likely to encounter, and the best way of acquiring a natural conversational rhythm is to act out the conversations using gestures and facial expressions while listening to the CD.

4. Check your understanding

Each lesson ends with some practice questions which you should use to check that you have correctly understood the lesson.

5. Apply what you have learnt

Try talking to Japanese people using the Japanese you have learnt. Applying what you have learnt right away, before you forget it, is the quickest way to progress.

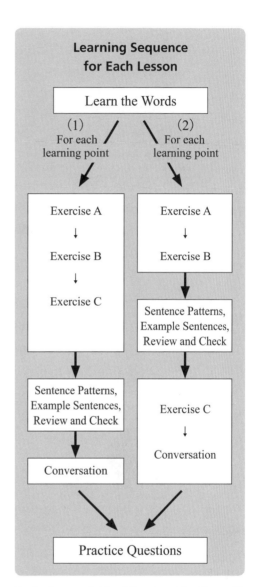

Study the material by following either Route (1) or Route (2). To make sure you cover all the key learning points, please check the Table of Key Learning Points at the end of this book.

CHARACTERS

Mike Miller

American, employee of IMC

Sato Keiko

Japanese, employee of IMC

Jose Santos

Brazilian, employee of Brazil Air

Maria Santos

Brazilian, housewife

Karina

Indonesian, student at Fuji University

Wang Xue

Chinese, doctor at Kobe Hospital

Yamada Ichiro

Japanese, employee of IMC

Yamada Tomoko

Japanese, bank clerk

Matsumoto Tadashi

Japanese,
department chief at IMC

Matsumoto Yoshiko

Japanese, housewife

Kimura Izumi

Japanese, announcer

John Watt

British,
professor at Sakura University

Karl Schmidt

German,
engineer at Power Electric Company

Lee Jin Ju

Korean,
research worker at AKC

Teresa Santos

Brazilian, schoolgirl (9 yrs.),
daughter of Jose and Maria Santos

Yamada Taro

Japanese, schoolboy (8 yrs.),
son of Ichiro and Tomoko Yamada

Gupta

Indian, employee of IMC

Thawaphon

Thai,
student at Japanese language school

※IMC（computer software company）
※AKC（アジア研究センター：Asia Research Institute）

CONTENTS

Lesson 1 ·· 10

Ⅰ. Vocabulary

Ⅱ. Translation
Sentence Patterns and Example Sentences
Conversation: **How do you do?**

Ⅲ. Useful Words and Information
Countries, People and Languages

Ⅳ. Grammar Notes
1. N₁ は N₂ です
2. N₁ は N₂ じゃ（では）ありません
3. N₁ は N₂ ですか
4. N も
5. N₁ の N₂
6. ～さん

Lesson 2 ·· 16

Ⅰ. Vocabulary

Ⅱ. Translation
Sentence Patterns and Example Sentences
Conversation:
Thank you in advance for your kindness

Ⅲ. Useful Words and Information
Family Names

Ⅳ. Grammar Notes
1. これ／それ／あれ
2. この N ／その N ／あの N
3. そうです
4. ～か、～か
5. N₁ の N₂
6. の substituting for a noun
7. お～
8. そうですか

GENERAL FEATURES OF JAPANESE

1. Parts of Speech   The Japanese language is composed of verbs, adjectives, nouns, adverbs, conjunctions, particles and other parts of speech.

2. Word Order   In Japanese, predicates always come at the end of a sentence. Modifiers always appear in front of the word(s) modified.

3. Predicates   Predicates are formed from verbs, adjectives, nouns and です（だ）. They inflect according to, for example, whether they are (1) affirmative or negative, (2) past or non-past. They do not inflect for person, gender or number.

4. Particles   Particles are used after a word or at the end of a sentence. They indicate relationships between words and add various meanings.

5. Omission   Subjects and objects are often omitted if they can be understood from the context.

JAPANESE WRITING

There are three types of script in Japanese: hiragana, katakana, and kanji (Chinese characters).

Hiragana and katakana are phonetic symbols purely representing sounds, while kanji are ideographs, conveying meanings as well as sounds.

Japanese is usually written with a combination of hiragana, katakana, and kanji, with katakana used to write foreign names and loanwords and hiragana used to write particles and the grammatical endings of verbs and adjectives.

Romaji (the letters of the Roman alphabet) are also occasionally used to write Japanese (the names of train stations are one example) for the convenience of foreigners.

Here are examples of all four types of script:

田中　さん　は　ミラー　さん　と　デパート　へ　行　きます。
○　　　□　　□　　△　　　□　　□　　△　　　□　○　　□

Mr. Tanaka is going to the department store with Mr. Miller.

大阪　Osaka
○　　☆

(○−kanji　□−hiragana　△−katakana　☆−romaji)

INTRODUCTION

I. Japanese Pronunciation

1. Kana and Mora

Japanese can be written phonetically in kana as shown below.

A 'mora' is a unit of sound equivalent in length to one Japanese kana (or two of the contracted sounds called yo-on, which are written with small kana).

The Japanese language is based on five vowel sounds: あ (a), い (i), う (u), え (e) and お (o), which are used alone or attached to either a consonant (e.g. k + a ＝ か) or to a consonant plus the semi-vowel 'y' (e.g. k + y + a ＝ きゃ) (the only exception being a special mora, ん, which is not followed by a vowel). All of these sounds are or more or less equal in length when spoken.

e.g.,

```
             ┌── hiragana
  あ  ア ─── katakana
  a  ──────── romaji
```

	あ -column	い -column	う -column	え -column	お -column
あ -row	あ ア a	い イ i	う ウ u	え エ e	お オ o
か -row k	か カ ka	き キ ki	く ク ku	け ケ ke	こ コ ko
さ -row s	さ サ sa	し シ shi	す ス su	せ セ se	そ ソ so
た -row t	た タ ta	ち チ chi	つ ツ tsu	て テ te	と ト to
な -row n	な ナ na	に ニ ni	ぬ ヌ nu	ね ネ ne	の ノ no
は -row h	は ハ ha	ひ ヒ hi	ふ フ fu	へ ヘ he	ほ ホ ho
ま -row m	ま マ ma	み ミ mi	む ム mu	め メ me	も モ mo
や -row y	や ヤ ya	(い イ) (i)	ゆ ユ yu	(え エ) (e)	よ ヨ yo
ら -row r	ら ラ ra	り リ ri	る ル ru	れ レ re	ろ ロ ro
わ -row w	わ ワ wa	(い イ) (i)	(う ウ) (u)	(え エ) (e)	を ヲ o
	ん ン n				

きゃ キャ kya	きゅ キュ kyu	きょ キョ kyo
しゃ シャ sha	しゅ シュ shu	しょ ショ sho
ちゃ チャ cha	ちゅ チュ chu	ちょ チョ cho
にゃ ニャ nya	にゅ ニュ nyu	にょ ニョ nyo
ひゃ ヒャ hya	ひゅ ヒュ hyu	ひょ ヒョ hyo
みゃ ミャ mya	みゅ ミュ myu	みょ ミョ myo
りゃ リャ rya	りゅ リュ ryu	りょ リョ ryo

	あ -column	い -column	う -column	え -column	お -column
が -row g	が ガ ga	ぎ ギ gi	ぐ グ gu	げ ゲ ge	ご ゴ go
ざ -row z	ざ ザ za	じ ジ ji	ず ズ zu	ぜ ゼ ze	ぞ ゾ zo
だ -row d	だ ダ da	ぢ ヂ ji	づ ヅ zu	で デ de	ど ド do
ば -row b	ば バ ba	び ビ bi	ぶ ブ bu	べ ベ be	ぼ ボ bo
ぱ -row p	ぱ パ pa	ぴ ピ pi	ぷ プ pu	ぺ ペ pe	ぽ ポ po

ぎゃ ギャ gya	ぎゅ ギュ gyu	ぎょ ギョ gyo
じゃ ジャ ja	じゅ ジュ ju	じょ ジョ jo
びゃ ビャ bya	びゅ ビュ byu	びょ ビョ byo
ぴゃ ピャ pya	ぴゅ ピュ pyu	ぴょ ピョ pyo

The katakana letters in the square on the right are not in the above table. They are used to write sounds which are not original Japanese sounds but are needed for use in loanwords.

	ウィ wi		ウェ we	ウォ wo
			シェ she
			チェ che
ツァ tsa			ツェ tse	ツォ tso
	ティ ti	トゥ tu	
ファ fa	フィ fi		フェ fe	フォ fo
			ジェ je
	ディ di	ドゥ du	
		デュ dyu	

3

2. Long vowels

The five vowel sounds mentioned earlier (あ , い , う , え and お) constitute short vowels in Japanese, but they can be doubled in length (to two moras) to form long vowels. The meaning of a word changes according to the length of its vowel(s).

e.g. おばさん (aunt) : おば<u>あ</u>さん (grandmother)

おじさん (uncle) : おじ<u>い</u>さん (grandfather)

ゆき (snow) : ゆ<u>う</u>き (courage)

え (picture) : え<u>え</u> (yes)

とる (take) : と<u>お</u>る (pass)

ここ (here) : こ<u>う</u>こ<u>う</u> (high school)

へや (room) : へ<u>い</u>や (plain)

カ<u>ー</u>ド (card) タクシ<u>ー</u> (taxi) ス<u>ー</u>パ<u>ー</u> (supermarket)

エスカレ<u>ー</u>タ<u>ー</u> (escalator) ノ<u>ー</u>ト (notebook)

〔Note〕

1) How to write long vowels in hiragana:

To lengthen the vowels of the あ -column, い -column and う -column, add「あ」「い」or「う」respectively.

To lengthen the vowels of the え -column, add「い」

(exceptions : ええ yes, ねえ I say, おねえさん elder sister, and others).

To lengthen the vowels of the お -column, add「う」

(exceptions : おおきい big, おおい many, とおい far, and others).

2) How to write long vowels in katakana:

To lengthen any vowel in katakana, add the symbol「ー」.

3. Pronunciation of ん

「 ん 」is one mora long and never appears at the beginning of a word. To make it easier to say, it is pronounced /n/, /m/ or /ŋ/ according to the sound that comes after it.

① Before sounds from the「た -row」「だ -row」,「ら -row」and「な -row」,

it is pronounced /n/,

e.g. は<u>ん</u>たい (opposite) う<u>ん</u>どう (sport) せ<u>ん</u>ろ (track)

み<u>ん</u>な (everyone).

② Before sounds from the「ば -row」,「ぱ -row」and「ま -row」, it is pronounced /m/,

e.g. し<u>ん</u>ぶん (newspaper) え<u>ん</u>ぴつ (pencil) う<u>ん</u>めい (destiny).

③ Before sounds from the「か -row」and「が -row」, it is pronounced /ŋ/,

e.g. て<u>ん</u>き (weather) け<u>ん</u>がく (study visit).

4. Pronunciation of っ

「っ」is one mora long and appears before sounds from the「か-row」,「さ -row」,「た -row」and「ぱ-row」. When used in writing loanwords, it is also used before sounds in the「ザ-row」,「ダ -row」, etc.

 e.g. ぶか(subordinate)：ぶっか (commodity price)

    かさい(fire)：かっさい(applause)

    おと(sound)：おっと(husband)

    にっき(diary)　ざっし(magazine)　きって(stamp)

    いっぱい(full)　コップ(glass)　ベッド(bed)

5. Contracted Sound

The sound represented by using one of the small hiragana letters「ゃ」「ゅ」and「ょ」 in combination with a full-sized hiragana letter is called a yo-on (contracted sound). Although written with two letters, these sounds are only one mora long.

 e.g. ひやく (jump)：ひゃく (hundred)

    じゆう (freedom)：じゅう (ten)

    びよういん (beauty salon)：びょういん (hospital)

    シャツ(shirt)　おちゃ (tea)　ぎゅうにゅう(milk)　きょう(today)

    ぶちょう (department head)　りょこう (travel)

6. Pronunciation of が-row

The consonants of the が-row pronounced [g] when they fall at the beginning of a word, and [ŋ] when they fall elsewhere. However, some people these days make no distinction between these two sounds and pronounce them [g] wherever they fall.

7. Devoicing of vowels

The vowels [i] and [u] tend to be devoiced and become silent when they fall between voiceless consonants (e.g. すき like). The final vowel [u] of「～です」and「～ます」 also tends to be silent (e.g. したいです want to do, ききます listen).

8. Accent

The Japanese language has pitch accent; that is, some moras in a word are pronounced high and others low. There are four types of accent, and the meaning of a word changes according to how it is accented.

The standard Japanese accent is characterised by the fact that the first and second moras have different pitches, and that the pitch never rises again once it has fallen.

Types of accent

① Flat (the pitch does not drop)

e.g. にわ (garden)　はな (nose)　なまえ (name)
にほんご (Japanese language)

② Beginning high (the pitch drops after the first mora)

e.g. ほん (book)　てんき (weather)　らいげつ (next month)

③ Middle high (the pitch drops after the second mora)

e.g. たまご (egg)　ひこうき (aeroplane)　せんせい (teacher)

④ Ending high (the pitch drops after the last mora)

e.g. くつ (shoes)　はな (flower)　やすみ (holiday)
おとうと (younger brother)

はな (nose) in ① and はな (flower) in ④ sound similar, but if the particle が is added after these they are accented differently, and ① is pronounced はなが while ④ is pronounced はなが. Here are some other examples of words whose meaning differs according to the type of accent:

はし (bridge) : はし (chopsticks)　　いち (one) : いち (position)

There are also local differences in accent. For example, the accent in the Osaka area is quite different from the standard accent. Here are some examples:

e.g.　Tokyo accent　　　：　　　Osaka accent
(standard Japanese accent)

はな : はな　　　(flower)
りんご : りんご　　　(apple)
おんがく : おんがく　　　(music)

9. Intonation

There are three patterns of intonation in Japanese: ① flat ② rising, and ③ falling. Questions are pronounced with a rising intonation. Other sentences are usually pronounced flat, but sometimes with a falling intonation. A falling intonation can express feelings such as agreement, disappointment, etc.

e.g.　佐藤(さとう)：　あした 友達(ともだち)と お花見(はなみ)を します。【→flat】
ミラーさんも いっしょに 行きませんか。【↗rising】
ミラー：いいですね。【↘falling】

Sato:　　I'm going to see the cherry blossoms tomorrow with some friends.
Would you like to come with us, Mr. Miller?

Miller:　That sounds good.

II. Classroom Language

1. 始めましょう。   Let's begin.

2. 終わりましょう。   Let's finish.

3. 休みましょう。   Let's take a break.

4. わかりますか。   Do you understand?
    ……はい、わかります。   ……Yes, I do.
    いいえ、わかりません。   No, I don't.

5. もう 一度 [お願いします]。   Once more [please].

6. いいです。   That's fine.

7. 違います。   No, that's wrong.

8. 名前   name

9. 試験、宿題   test, homework

10. 質問、答え、例   question, answer, example

III. Everyday Greetings and Expressions

1. おはよう ございます。   Good morning.

2. こんにちは。   Hello.

3. こんばんは。   Good evening.

4. お休みなさい。   Good night.

5. さようなら。   Goodbye.

6. ありがとう ございます。   Thank you.

7. すみません。   Excuse me./Sorry.

8. お願いします。   Please.

TERMS USED FOR INSTRUCTION

第一課	Lesson -	フォーム	form
文型	Sentence Pattern	〜形	〜 form
例文	Example Sentence	修飾	modification
会話	Conversation	例外	exception
練習	Exercise		
問題	Practice Question	名詞	noun
答え	Answer	動詞	verb
読み物	Text	形容詞	adjective
復習	Review	い形容詞	い-adjective
		な形容詞	な-adjective
目次	Contents	助詞	particle
		副詞	adverb
索引	Index	接続詞	conjunction
		数詞	numeral
文法	grammar	助数詞	counter suffix
文	sentence	疑問詞	interrogative
単語(語)	word	名詞文	noun (predicate) sentence
句	phrase		
節	clause	動詞文	verb (predicate) sentence
発音	pronunciation	形容詞文	adjective (predicate) sentence
母音	vowel		
子音	consonant		
拍	mora	主語	subject
アクセント	accent	述語	predicate
イントネーション	intonation	目的語	object
		主題	topic
[か]行	[か]row	こうてい 肯定	affirmative
[い]列	[い]column	否定	negative
		完了	perfective
丁寧体	polite style of speech	未完了	imperfective
普通体	plain style of speech	過去	past
活用	inflection, conjugation	非過去	non-past

8

KEY TO SYMBOLS AND ABBREVIATIONS

1. Symbols Used in I. Vocabulary

① ～ indicates a missing word or phrase

    e.g. ～から 来ました。　came from ～

② － indicates a missing number

    e.g. －歳　　－ years old

③ Words and phrases that can be omitted are enclosed in square brackets:

    e.g. どうぞ よろしく ［お願いします］。　Pleased to meet you.

④ Synonymous words and phrases are enclosed in round brackets:

    e.g. だれ（どなた）　who

⑤ Words marked with a star（＊）are not used in that lesson but are presented as being relevant.

⑥ The Exercise C section（〈練習 C〉）presents expressions used in the lesson's Exercise C.

⑦ The Conversation section（〈会話〉）presents words and expressions used in the lesson's Conversation.

2. Abbreviations Used in IV. Grammar Notes

N	noun（名詞）	e.g. がくせい（student）　つくえ（desk）
い-adj	い-adjective（い形容詞）	e.g. おいしい（delicious） 　　　たかい（high, expensive）
な-adj	な-adjective（な形容詞）	e.g. きれい［な］（beautiful） 　　　しずか［な］（quiet）
V	verb（動詞）	e.g. かきます（write）　たべます（eat）
S	sentence（文）	e.g. これは 本です。　This is a book. わたしは あした 東京 へ 行きます。 I'm going to Tokyo tomorrow.

Lesson 1

I. Vocabulary

わたし		I
あなた		you
あの ひと（あの かた）	あの 人（あの 方）	that person, he, she（あの かた is the polite equivalent of あの ひと）
～さん		Mr., Ms.（suffix added to a name for expressing politeness）
～ちゃん		（suffix often added to a child's name instead of ～さん）
～じん	～人	（suffix meaning 'a national of'; e.g. アメリカじん, an American）
せんせい	先生	teacher, instructor（not used when referring to one's own job）
きょうし	教師	teacher, instructor
がくせい	学生	student
かいしゃいん	会社員	company employee
しゃいん	社員	employee of ～ company（used with a company's name, e.g. IMC の しゃいん）
ぎんこういん	銀行員	bank employee
いしゃ	医者	[medical] doctor
けんきゅうしゃ	研究者	researcher, scholar
だいがく	大学	university
びょういん	病院	hospital
だれ（どなた）		who（どなた is the polite equivalent of だれ）
－さい	－歳	－ years old
なんさい（おいくつ）	何歳	how old（おいくつ is the polite equivalent of なんさい）
はい		yes
いいえ		no

〈練習 C〉

初めまして。	How do you do? (lit. I am meeting you for the first time. Usually used as the first phrase when introducing oneself.)
～から 来ました。	I'm from ～ (country).
[どうぞ] よろしく [お願いします]。	Pleased to meet you. (lit. Please be nice to me. Usually used at the end of a self-introduction.)
失礼ですが	Excuse me, but (used when asking someone for personal information such as their name or address)
お名前は?	May I have your name?
こちらは ～さんです。	This is Mr./Ms. ～.

....

アメリカ	U.S.A.
イギリス	U.K.
インド	India
インドネシア	Indonesia
韓国	South Korea
タイ	Thailand
中国	China
ドイツ	Germany
日本	Japan
ブラジル	Brazil

IMC／パワー電気／ブラジルエアー	fictitious companies
AKC	a fictitious institute
神戸病院	a fictitious hospital
さくら大学／富士大学	fictitious universities

II. Translation

Sentence Patterns

1. I'm Mike Miller.
2. Mr. Santos isn't a student.
3. Is Mr. Miller a company employee?
4. Mr. Santos is also a company employee.

Example Sentences

1. Are you [Mr.] Mike Miller?
   ······Yes, I am [Mike Miller].

2. Are you a student, Mr. Miller?
   ······No, I'm not [a student].

3. Is Mr. Wang a bank employee?
   ······No, he isn't [a bank employee]. He's a doctor.

4. Who's that [person]?
   ······That's Professor Watt. He's at Sakura University.

5. Is Mr. Gupta a company employee?
   ······Yes, he is [a company employee].
   Is Karina a company employee, too?
   ······No, she's a student.

6. How old is Teresa?
   ······She's nine [years old].

Conversation

How do you do?

Sato: Good morning.
Yamada: Good morning.
           Ms. Sato, this is Mike Miller.
Miller: How do you do?
           I'm Mike Miller.
           I'm from America.
           Pleased to meet you.
Sato: I'm Keiko Sato.
           Nice to meet you.

III. Useful Words and Information

国・人・ことば　Countries, People and Languages

国　Country	人　People	ことば　Language
アメリカ (U.S.A.)	アメリカ人	英語 (English)
イギリス (U.K.)	イギリス人	英語 (English)
イタリア (Italy)	イタリア人	イタリア語 (Italian)
イラン (Iran)	イラン人	ペルシア語 (Persian)
インド (India)	インド人	ヒンディー語 (Hindi)
インドネシア (Indonesia)	インドネシア人	インドネシア語 (Indonesian)
エジプト (Egypt)	エジプト人	アラビア語 (Arabic)
オーストラリア (Australia)	オーストラリア人	英語 (English)
カナダ (Canada)	カナダ人	英語 (English) フランス語 (French)
韓国 (South Korea)	韓国人	韓国語 (Korean)
サウジアラビア (Saudi Arabia)	サウジアラビア人	アラビア語 (Arabic)
シンガポール (Singapore)	シンガポール人	英語 (English)
スペイン (Spain)	スペイン人	スペイン語 (Spanish)
タイ (Thailand)	タイ人	タイ語 (Thai)
中国 (China)	中国人	中国語 (Chinese)
ドイツ (Germany)	ドイツ人	ドイツ語 (German)
日本 (Japan)	日本人	日本語 (Japanese)
フランス (France)	フランス人	フランス語 (French)
フィリピン (Philippines)	フィリピン人	フィリピノ語 (Filipino)
ブラジル (Brazil)	ブラジル人	ポルトガル語 (Portuguese)
ベトナム (Vietnam)	ベトナム人	ベトナム語 (Vietnamese)
マレーシア (Malaysia)	マレーシア人	マレーシア語 (Malaysian)
メキシコ (Mexico)	メキシコ人	スペイン語 (Spanish)
ロシア (Russia)	ロシア人	ロシア語 (Russian)

IV. Grammar Notes

1. $\boxed{\text{N}_1 \text{ は N}_2 \text{ です}}$

1) Particle は

The particle は indicates that the noun before it (N₁) is the topic of the sentence (see Topic and Subject article). The speaker forms a sentence by adding は to what he or she wants to talk about, and then makes statements about it.

① わたしは マイク・ミラーです。   I'm Mike Miller.

[Note] The particle は is read わ.

2) です

Nouns used with です work as predicates. Besides indicating judgment or assertion, です also shows politeness towards the listener. です inflects when the sentence is negative (see 2. below) or in the past tense (see Lesson 12).

② わたしは 会社員です。   I'm a company employee.

2. $\boxed{\text{N}_1 \text{ は N}_2 \text{ じゃ（では）ありません}}$

じゃ（では）ありません is the negative form of です. じゃ ありません is often used in everyday conversation, while では ありません is used in formal speech and writing.

③ サントスさんは 学生じゃ ありません。   Mr. Santos isn't a student.
     （では）

[Note] The は in では is pronounced わ.

3. $\boxed{\text{N}_1 \text{ は N}_2 \text{ ですか}}$ (question)

1) Particle か

The particle か is used to express uncertainty, doubt, etc. on the part of the speaker. A question can be formed simply by adding か to the end of a sentence. A question usually ends with a rising intonation.

2) Questions asking whether a statement is correct or not

This type of question is formed simply by adding か to the end of the statement, leaving the word order the same. The reply begins with はい if the statement is agreed with, and いいえ if it is disagreed with.

④ ミラーさんは アメリカ人ですか。   Is Mr. Miller an American?
     ……はい、アメリカ人です。   ……Yes, he is [an American].

⑤ ミラーさんは 先生ですか。   Is Mr. Miller a teacher?
     ……いいえ、先生じゃ ありません。   ……No, he isn't [a teacher].

3) Questions with interrogatives

An interrogative replaces the part of the sentence that states what the speaker wants to ask about. The word order does not change, and か is added at the end.

⑥ あの 方は どなたですか。   Who's that [person]?
     ……[あの 方は] ミラーさんです。   ……That's Mr. Miller.

4. $\boxed{\text{N も}}$

「も」 is used when the same thing applies as was stated previously.

⑦ ミラーさんは 会社員です。グプタさんも 会社員です。

    Mr. Miller is a company employee. Mr Gupta is also a company employee.

5. $\boxed{\text{N}_1 \text{ の } \text{N}_2}$

When a noun N_1 modifies a following noun N_2, の is used to connect the two nouns. In Lesson 1, N_1 represents an organisation or some kind of group to which N_2 belongs.

⑧ ミラーさんは IMC の 社員です。   Mr. Miller is an IMC employee.

6. $\boxed{\text{〜さん}}$

さん is added to the given name or family name of the listener or a third person to show the speaker's respect to that person. It should never be used with the speaker's own name. ちゃん is added to small children's names instead of さん to indicate familiarity.

⑨ あの 方は ミラーさんです。   That's Mr. Miller.

When referring directly to the listener, the word あなた (you) is not generally used if the speaker knows the listener's name. The listener's given name or family name followed by さん is usually used.

⑩ 鈴木： ミラーさんは 学生ですか。 Suzuki: Are you a student, Mr. Miller?
   ミラー： いいえ、会社員です。 Miller: No, I work for a company.

[Note] あなた is used to address someone with whom one is very familiar, such as one's husband, wife, romantic partner, etc. Be careful about using it in other situations, as it can sound impolite.

15

Lesson 2

I. Vocabulary

これ		this (thing here)
それ		that (thing near the listener)
あれ		that (thing over there)
この ～		this ～, this ～ here
その ～*		that ～, that ～ near the listener
あの ～*		that ～, that ～ over there
ほん	本	book
じしょ	辞書	dictionary
ざっし	雑誌	magazine
しんぶん	新聞	newspaper
ノート		notebook
てちょう	手帳	personal organiser
めいし	名刺	business card
カード		(credit) card
えんぴつ	鉛筆	pencil
ボールペン		ballpoint pen
シャープペンシル		mechanical pencil, propelling pencil
かぎ		key
とけい	時計	watch, clock
かさ	傘	umbrella
かばん		bag, briefcase
CD		CD, compact disc
テレビ		television
ラジオ		radio
カメラ		camera
コンピューター		computer
くるま	車	car, vehicle
つくえ	机	desk
いす		chair
チョコレート		chocolate
コーヒー		coffee

[お]みやげ	[お]土産	souvenir, present
えいご	英語	the English language
にほんご	日本語	the Japanese language
～ご	～語	～ language
なん	何	what
そう		so

〈練習 C〉

あのう	Er... (used to show hesitation)
えっ	Oh? What! (used when hearing something unexpected)
どうぞ。	Here you are. (used when offering someone something)
[どうも] ありがとう [ございます]。	Thank you [very much].
そうですか。	I see.
違います。	No, it isn't./You are wrong.
あ	Oh! (used when becoming aware of something)

〈会話〉

これから お世話に なります。	Thank you in advance for your kindness.
こちらこそ [どうぞ] よろしく [お願いします]。	Pleased to meet you, too. (response to [どうぞ] よろしく [おねがいします]。)

II. Translation

Sentence Patterns
1. This is a dictionary.
2. That's my umbrella.
3. This book is mine.

Example Sentences
1. Is this a ballpoint pen?
   ······Yes, it is.

2. Is that a notebook?
   ······No, it's a personal organiser.

3. What's that?
   ······It's a business card.

4. Is this a 9, or a 7?
   ······It's a 9.

5. What kind of magazine is that?
   ······It's a computer magazine.

6. Whose bag is that?
   ······It's Ms. Sato's [bag].

7. Is this yours, Mr. Miller?
   ······No, it's not [mine].

8. Whose is this key?
   ······It's mine.

Conversation

Thank you in advance for your kindness

Ichiro Yamada:	Yes, who is it?
Santos:	It's Jose Santos, from 408.

....

Santos:	Hello, I'm Jose Santos.
	I've just moved in here. (lit: Thank you in advance for your kindness.)
	Nice to meet you.
Ichiro Yamada:	Pleased to meet you, too.
Santos:	Here's some coffee for you. (lit: Umm...... this is coffee. Please take it.)
Ichiro Yamada:	Thank you very much.

III. Useful Words and Information

名前　　Family Names

Common Family Names in Japanese

1	佐藤	2	鈴木	3	高橋	4	田中
5	渡辺	6	伊藤	7	山本	8	中村
9	小林	10	加藤	11	吉田	12	山田
13	佐々木	14	斎藤	15	山口	16	松本
17	井上	18	木村	19	林	20	清水

城岡啓二、村山忠重「日本の姓の全国順位データベース」より。2011 年 8 月公開
Taken from 'A Database of the Nationwide Order of Prevalence of Japanese Family Names',
by Keiji Shirooka and Tadashige Murayama August 2011

Greetings

初めまして。

⇦ When people meet for the first time on business, business cards are exchanged.

どうぞ よろしく お願いします。

When you move house, it is polite to introduce yourself to your new neighbours and give them a ⇨ small gift, such as a towel, soap or sweets.

IV. Grammar Notes

2

1. これ／それ／あれ

これ, それ and あれ are demonstratives and work as nouns.

これ refers to something near the speaker.

それ refers to something near the listener.

あれ refers to something distant from both the speaker and the listener.

① それは 辞書ですか。 　　　　Is that a dictionary?

② これは だれの 傘ですか。 　　Whose umbrella is this?

2. この N／その N／あの N

この, その and あの modify nouns.

③ この 本は わたしのです。 　　This book is mine.

④ あの 方は どなたですか。 　　Who is that [person]?

これ
この かばん

それ
その かばん

あれ
あの かばん

3. そうです

In a noun sentence, the wordそう is often used to answer (in the affirmative) a question requiring an affirmative or negative answer. The expression はい、そうです can be used.

⑤ それは 辞書ですか。 　　　　Is that a dictionary?

　……はい、そうです。 　　　　……Yes, it is.

そう is not usually used when answering a question in the negative; it is more common to say ちがいます (No, it isn't), followed by the correct answer.

⑥ それは ミラーさんのですか。 　　Is that Mr. Miller's?

　……いいえ、違います。 　　　　……No, it isn't.

⑦ それは シャープペンシルですか。 　Is that a mechanical pencil?

　……いいえ、ボールペンです。 　　……No, it's a ballpoint pen.

4. ～か、～か

This is a question asking the listener to choose between two or more alternatives for the answer. In answering this type of question, it is usual to state the chosen alternative, without saying either はい or いいえ.

⑧　これは「9」ですか、「7」ですか。　　　Is this a 9 or a 7?
　　……「9」です。　　　　　　　　　　　　……It's a 9.

5. N₁ の N₂

It was explained in Lesson 1 that の is used to connect two nouns N₁ and N₂ when N₁ modifies N₂. The present lesson explains some other uses of の.

1) N₁ explains what N₂ is about.

⑨　これは コンピューターの 本です。　　This is a book on computers.

2) N₁ indicates who owns N₂.

⑩　これは わたしの 本です。　　　　　This is my book.

6. の substituting for a noun

の can be used instead of a noun that has already been mentioned (e.g. instead of かばん in example ⑪). If placed after the noun (as in example ⑪ , where it comes after the noun さとうさん), it enables N₂ （かばん）in N₁ の N₂ （さとうさんの かばん） to be omitted. の is used as a replacement for things but not for people.

⑪　あれは だれの かばんですか。　　　　Whose bag is that?
　　……佐藤さんのです。　　　　　　　　　……It's Ms. Sato's.

⑫　この かばんは あなたのですか。　　　　Is this bag yours?
　　……いいえ、わたしのじゃ ありません。　……No, it isn't [mine].

⑬　ミラーさんは IMC の 社員ですか。　　Does Mr. Miller work at IMC?
　　……はい、IMC の 社員です。　　　　……Yes, he does.
　　×　はい、IMC のです。

7. お～

The prefix お is attached to words when the speaker is speaking politely
(e.g. ［お］みやげ、［お］さけ).

8. そうですか

This expression is used by the speaker to acknowledge some new information he or she has just been given. It is pronounced with a falling intonation.

⑭　この 傘は あなたのですか。　　　　　　Is this umbrella yours?
　　……いいえ、違います。シュミットさんのです。　……No, it isn't. It's Mr Schmidt's.
　　そうですか。　　　　　　　　　　　　　　Oh, I see.

Lesson 3

I. Vocabulary

ここ		here, this place
そこ		there, that place near the listener
あそこ		that place over there
どこ		where, what place
こちら		this way, this place (polite equivalent of ここ)
そちら		that way, that place near the listener (polite equivalent of そこ)
あちら		that way, that place over there (polite equivalent of あそこ)
どちら		which way, where (polite equivalent of どこ)
きょうしつ	教室	classroom
しょくどう	食堂	dining hall, canteen
じむしょ	事務所	office
かいぎしつ	会議室	conference room, meeting room
うけつけ	受付	reception desk
ロビー		lobby
へや	部屋	room
トイレ（おてあらい）	（お手洗い）	toilet, rest room
かいだん	階段	staircase
エレベーター		lift, elevator
エスカレーター		escalator
じどうはんばいき	自動販売機	vending machine
でんわ	電話	telephone handset, telephone call
［お］くに	［お］国	country
かいしゃ	会社	company
うち		house, home

くつ	靴	shoes
ネクタイ		tie, necktie
ワイン		wine

うりば	売り場	department, counter (in a department store, etc.)
ちか	地下	basement
ーかい（がい）	一階	-th floor
なんがい*	何階	what floor

| ーえん | 一円 | － yen |
| いくら | | how much |

ひゃく	百	hundred
せん	千	thousand
まん	万	ten thousand

〈練習 C〉

| すみません。 | Excuse me. |
| どうも。 | Thanks. |

〈会話〉

いらっしゃいませ。	Welcome./May I help you? (a greeting to a customer or a guest entering a shop, etc.)
[〜を] 見せて ください。	Please show me [〜].
じゃ	well, then, in that case
[〜を] ください。	Give me [〜], please.

....

イタリア	Italy
スイス	Switzerland
フランス	France
ジャカルタ	Jakarta
バンコク	Bangkok
ベルリン	Berlin
新大阪	name of a station in Osaka

II. Translation

Sentence Patterns
1. This is the cafeteria.
2. The elevator's over there.

Example Sentences
1. Is this Shin-Osaka?
   ……Yes, it is.

2. Where's the toliet?
   ……It's over there.

3. Where's Mr. Yamada?
   ……He's in the meeting room.

4. Where's the office?
   ……It's over there.

5. Which country are you from?
   ……America.

6. Where are those shoes from?
   ……They're Italian [shoes].

7. How much is this watch?
   ……It's 18,600 yen.

Conversation

I'll take it, please

Shop Assistant A:	Good afternoon. (lit: Welcome.)
Maria:	[Excuse me.] Where's the wine department?
Shop Assistant A:	It's on Basement Level 1.
Maria:	Thanks.

……………………………………………………………

Maria:	Excuse me. Could you show me that bottle of wine, please?
Shop Assistant B:	Yes, here you are.
Maria:	Where's this wine from?
Shop Assistant B:	It's from Japan.
Maria:	How much is it?
Shop Assistant B:	It's 2,500 yen.
Maria:	OK, I'll take it, please.

III. Useful Words and Information

デパート　　Department Store

屋上（おくじょう）	遊園地（ゆうえんち） amusement area	
8階（かい）	レストラン・催し物会場（もよおし ものかいじょう） restaurants, event hall	
7階（かい）	時計（とけい）・眼鏡（めがね） watches, spectacles	
6階（かい）	スポーツ用品（ようひん）・旅行用品（りょこうようひん） sporting goods, leisure goods	
5階（かい）	子（こ）ども服（ふく）・おもちゃ・本（ほん）・文房具（ぶんぼうぐ） children's clothes, toys, books, stationery	
4階（かい）	家具（かぐ）・食器（しょっき）・電化製品（でんかせいひん） furniture, kitchenware, electrical appliances	
3階（かい）	紳士服（しんしふく） men's wear	
2階（かい）	婦人服（ふじんふく） ladies' wear	
1階（かい）	靴（くつ）・かばん・アクセサリー・化粧品（けしょうひん） shoes, bags, accessories, cosmetics	
地下（ちか）1階（かい）	食品（しょくひん） food	
地下（ちか）2階（かい）	駐車場（ちゅうしゃじょう） car park, parking lot	

3

25

IV. Grammar Notes

1. こ こ ／そ こ ／あ そ こ ／こ ち ら ／そ ち ら ／あ ち ら

The demonstratives こ こ, そ こ and あ そ こ
refer to places. こ こ indicates the place
where the speaker is, そ こ the place where
the listener is, and あ そ こ a place distant
from both the speaker and the listener.
こ ち ら, そ ち ら and あ ち ら refer to direction
and can also be used as politer-sounding
alternatives for こ こ, そ こ and あ そ こ.

[Note] When the speaker regards the
listener as sharing his/her territory, the
place where they both are is designated by
こ こ. In this situation, そ こ indicates a
place slightly distant from where they both
are, and あ そ こ somewhere even further
away.

2. N は place です

Using this sentence pattern, you can state where a place, thing or person is.

① お手洗いは あそこです。　　　　The toilet is over there.
② 電話は 2階です。　　　　　　　The telephone is on the second floor.
③ 山田さんは 事務所です。　　　　Mr. Yamada is in his office.

3. ど こ ／ど ち ら

ど こ is used for asking "Where?" and ど ち ら for "Which direction?" ど ち ら can also
be used for asking "Where?", in which case it is politer than ど こ .

④ お手洗いは どこですか。　　　　Where's the toilet?
　　……あそこです。　　　　　　　……It's over there.
⑤ エレベーターは どちらですか。　Where's the lift?
　　……あちらです。　　　　　　　……It's in that direction. (It's over there.)

3

26

どこ and どちら are also used for asking the name of the country, company, school or other place or organisation to which someone belongs. なん cannot be used in this case. どちら is politer than どこ.

⑥ 学校（がっこう）は どこですか。　　　　　What school do you go to?

⑦ 会社（かいしゃ）は どちらですか。　　　　What company do you work for?

4. | N₁ の N₂ |

When N₁ is the name of a country and N₂ is the name of a product, it means that N₂ is made in that country. When N₁ is the name of a company and N₂ is the name of a product, it means that N₂ is made by that company. The interrogative どこ is used when asking where or by what company something is made.

⑧ これは どこの コンピューターですか。　　Where is this computer made? / What company is this computer made by?

……日本（にほん）の コンピューターです。　　……It's made in Japan.

……パワー電気（でんき）の コンピューターです。

……It's made by Power Electric Company.

5. The こ／そ／あ／ど system of demonstratives

	こ series	そ series	あ series	ど series
Thing	これ	それ	あれ	どれ （L.16）
Thing / Person	この N	その N	あの N	どの N （L.16）
Place	ここ	そこ	あそこ	どこ
Direction / Place (polite)	こちら	そちら	あちら	どちら

6. | お～ |

The prefix お is added to things related to the listener or a third party in order to show the speaker's respect toward that person.

⑨ ［お］国（くに）は どちらですか。　　　　What country are you from?

Lesson 4

I. Vocabulary

おきます	起きます	get up, wake up
ねます	寝ます	sleep, go to bed
はたらきます	働きます	work
やすみます	休みます	take a rest, take a holiday
べんきょうします	勉強します	study
おわります	終わります	finish
デパート		department store
ぎんこう	銀行	bank
ゆうびんきょく	郵便局	post office
としょかん	図書館	library
びじゅつかん	美術館	art museum, art gallery
いま	今	now
―じ	―時	― o'clock
―ふん（―ぷん）	―分	― minute
はん	半	half
なんじ	何時	what time
なんぷん*	何分	what minute
ごぜん	午前	a.m., morning
ごご	午後	p.m., afternoon
あさ	朝	morning
ひる	昼	daytime, noon
ばん（よる）	晩（夜）	night, evening
おととい		the day before yesterday
きのう		yesterday
きょう		today
あした		tomorrow
あさって		the day after tomorrow
けさ		this morning
こんばん	今晩	this evening, tonight
やすみ	休み	rest, a holiday, a day off
ひるやすみ	昼休み	lunchtime

しけん	試験	examination, test
かいぎ	会議	meeting, conference（～を します： hold a meeting）
えいが	映画	film, movie
まいあさ	毎朝	every morning
まいばん	毎晩	every night
まいにち	毎日	every day
げつようび	月曜日	Monday
かようび	火曜日	Tuesday
すいようび	水曜日	Wednesday
もくようび	木曜日	Thursday
きんようび	金曜日	Friday
どようび	土曜日	Saturday
にちようび	日曜日	Sunday
なんようび	何曜日	what day of the week
～から		from ～
～まで		up to ～, until ～
～と ～		and（used to connect nouns）

II. Translation

Sentence Patterns
1. It's five past four now.
2. I get up at six [o'clock] every morning.
3. I studied yesterday.

Example Sentences
1. What time is it now?
······It's ten past two.
What's the time in New York now?
······It's ten past midnight.

2. What days are you off work?
······Saturdays and Sundays.

3. What are Apple Bank's opening hours?
······From nine till three.

4. What time do you usually go to bed?
······[I go to bed at] eleven o'clock.

5. When do you start and finish studying every day?
······I study from nine am until three pm.

6. Do you work on Saturdays?
······No, I don't.

7. Did you study yesterday?
······No, I didn't.

Conversation

What time are you open to?

Miller:	Excuse me, what is Asuka's phone number?
Sato:	Asuka? It's 5275-2725.
Miller:	Thank you very much.

....

'Asuka' staff member:	Hello, Asuka here.
Miller:	Excuse me. What time are you open to?
'Asuka' staff member:	Until ten.
Miller:	What days of the week are you closed?
'Asuka' staff member:	Sundays.
Miller:	I see. Thank you.

III. Useful Words and Information

<ruby>電話<rt>でんわ</rt></ruby>・<ruby>手紙<rt>てがみ</rt></ruby>　　**Telephone and Letters**

How to Use a Public Telephone

① Lift the receiver.

② Put coins or a card into the slot.

③ Press the numbers. *

④ Hang up the receiver.

⑤ Take card or change (if any).

Public telephones accept only ￥10 coins, ￥100 coins, and telephone cards.

If you put in a ￥100 coin, no change will be returned.

* If the machine has a start button, press it after ③.

Emergency and Information Numbers

110	<ruby>警察署<rt>けいさつしょ</rt></ruby>	police
119	<ruby>消防署<rt>しょうぼうしょ</rt></ruby>	fire/ambulance
117	<ruby>時報<rt>じほう</rt></ruby>	time
177	<ruby>天気予報<rt>てんきよほう</rt></ruby>	weather forecast
104	<ruby>電話番号案内<rt>でんわばんごうあんない</rt></ruby>	directory inquiries

---

How to Write an Address

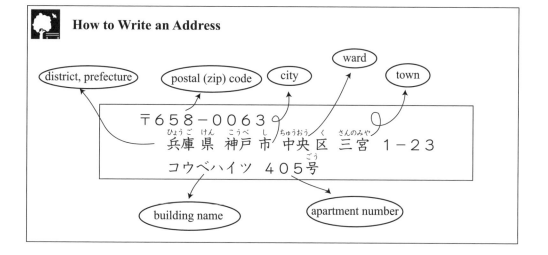

district, prefecture　　postal (zip) code　　city　　ward　　town

〒658−0063

<ruby>兵庫<rt>ひょうご</rt></ruby> <ruby>県<rt>けん</rt></ruby> <ruby>神戸<rt>こうべ</rt></ruby> <ruby>市<rt>し</rt></ruby> <ruby>中央<rt>ちゅうおう</rt></ruby> <ruby>区<rt>く</rt></ruby> <ruby>三宮<rt>さんのみや</rt></ruby> 1−23

コウベハイツ 405<ruby>号<rt>ごう</rt></ruby>

building name　　apartment number

4

IV. Grammar Notes

1. 今 ー時ー分です

To express time, the counter suffixes 時 (o'clock) and 分 (minutes) are placed after the numbers. 分 is read ふん after 2, 5, 7, or 9 and ぷん after 1, 3, 4, 6, 8 and 10. 1, 6, 8 and 10 are read いっ, ろっ, はっ, and じゅっ（じっ）before ぷん (see Appendix).
To ask the time, なん is placed in front of じ or ぷん.

① 今 何時ですか。 　　　　　　　　What time is it now?
　……7時10分です。 　　　　　　　　……It's 7:10.

2. Ｖ ます／Ｖ ません／Ｖ ました／Ｖ ませんでした

1) Ｖ ます works as a predicate. Using ます shows politeness toward the listener.
② わたしは 毎日 勉強します。 　　I study every day.

2) Ｖ ます is used when a sentence expresses something habitual or a truth. It is also used when a sentence expresses a behavior or event that will occur in the future. The table below shows its negative and past-tense forms.

	Non-past (future/present)	Past
Affirmative	おきます	おきました
Negative	おきません	おきませんでした

③ 毎朝 6時に 起きます。 　　　　I get up at six every morning.

④ あした 6時に 起きます。 　　　　I'm going to get up at six tomorrow morning.

⑤ けさ 6時に 起きました。 　　　　I got up at six this morning.

3) Verb question sentences are formed by putting か at the end of the sentence, without changing the word order. When using an interrogative, this is placed in the part of the sentence that the speaker wants to ask about. When answering such questions, the verb in the question is repeated. そうです and ちがいます（see Lesson 2）cannot be used when replying to a verb sentence question.

⑥ きのう 勉強しましたか。 　　　Did you study yesterday?
　……はい、勉強しました。 　　　　……Yes, I did [study].
　……いいえ、勉強しませんでした。 ……No, I didn't [study].

⑦ 毎朝 何時に 起きますか。 　　　What time do you get up in the mornings?
　……6時に 起きます。 　　　　　　……[I get up at] six o'clock.

3. Ｎ(time)に Ｖ

The particle に is appended to a noun indicating time to indicate the time of occurrence of an action.

⑧ 6時半に 起きます。 　　　　　　I get up at six-thirty.

⑨ ７月２日に 日本へ 来ました。

I came to Japan on the second of July. (See Lesson 5.)

[Note 1] に is not used with the following kinds of noun expressing time:

きょう，あした，あさって，きのう，おととい，けさ，こんばん，いま，まいあさ，まいばん，まいにち，せんしゅう(L.5)，こんしゅう(L.5)，らいしゅう(L.5)，いつ(L.5)，せんげつ(L.5)，こんげつ(L.5)，らいげつ(L.5)，ことし(L.5)，らいねん(L.5)，きょねん(L.5), etc.

⑩ きのう 勉強 しました。　　　　　　I studied yesterday.

[Note 2] With the following nouns, the use of に is optional:

〜ようび，あさ，ひる，ばん，よる

⑪ 日曜日[に] 奈良へ 行きます。

I'm going to Nara on Sunday. (See Lesson 5.)

4. | N₁ から N₂ まで |

1) から indicates a starting time or place, and まで indicates a finishing time or place.

⑫ ９時から ５時まで 勉強 します。　　I study from 9 to 5.

⑬ 大阪から 東京まで ３時間 かかります。

It takes three hours from Osaka to Tokyo. (See Lesson 11.)

2) から and まで are not always used together.

⑭ ９時から 働きます。　　　　　　I start work at nine.

3) To indicate the starting or finishing time/date of a noun introduced as a topic, 〜から、〜まで、or 〜から〜まで can be used with「です」attached.

⑮ 銀行は ９時から ３時までです。　　The bank's open from 9 to 3.

⑯ 昼休みは 12時からです。　　　　The lunch break starts at 12.

5. | N₁ と N₂ |

The particle と connects two nouns in coordinate relation.

⑰ 銀行の 休みは 土曜日と 日曜日です。

The bank is closed on Saturdays and Sundays.

6. | 〜ね |

The particle ね is attached to the end of a sentence and is used to elicit agreement from the listener, check that the listener has understood, or emphasize something to the listener.

⑱ 毎日 10時まで 勉強 します。　　I study till ten every day.
　……大変ですね。　　　　　　　……That's tough, isn't it?

⑲ 山田さんの 電話番号は 871の 6813 です。

Mr. Yamada's telephone number is 871-6813.

　……871の 6813ですね。　　　　……871-6813, right?

Lesson 5

I. Vocabulary

いきます	行きます	go
きます	来ます	come
かえります	帰ります	go home, return
がっこう	学校	school
スーパー		supermarket
えき	駅	station
ひこうき	飛行機	aeroplane, airplane
ふね	船	ship
でんしゃ	電車	electric train
ちかてつ	地下鉄	underground, subway
しんかんせん	新幹線	the Shinkansen, the bullet train
バス		bus
タクシー		taxi
じてんしゃ	自転車	bicycle
あるいて	歩いて	on foot
ひと	人	person, people
ともだち	友達	friend
かれ*	彼	he, boyfriend, lover
かのじょ	彼女	she, girlfriend, lover
かぞく	家族	family
ひとりで	一人で	alone, by oneself
せんしゅう	先週	last week
こんしゅう	今週	this week
らいしゅう	来週	next week
せんげつ	先月	last month
こんげつ*	今月	this month
らいげつ	来月	next month
きょねん	去年	last year
ことし*		this year
らいねん	来年	next year
ーねん*	一年	-th year
なんねん*	何年	what year
ーがつ	一月	-th month of the year
なんがつ*	何月	what month

ついたち	1 日	first day of the month
ふつか*	2 日	second, two days
みっか	3 日	third, three days
よっか*	4 日	fourth, four days
いつか*	5 日	fifth, five days
むいか	6 日	sixth, six days
なのか*	7 日	seventh, seven days
ようか*	8 日	eighth, eight days
ここのか	9 日	ninth, nine days
とおか	10 日	tenth, ten days
じゅうよっか	14 日	fourteenth, fourteen days
はつか*	20 日	twentieth, twenty days
にじゅうよっか*	24 日	twenty-fourth, twenty-four days
―にち	―日	-th day of the month, ― day(s)
なんにち*	何日	which day of the month, how many days

いつ		when

たんじょうび	誕生日	birthday

〈練習 C〉

そうですね。	Yes, it is.

〈会話〉

［どうも］ありがとう ございました。	Thank you very much.
どう いたしまして。	You're welcome./Don't mention it.
一番線	platform ― , -th platform
次の	next
普通	local (train)
急行*	rapid
特急*	express

....

甲子園	name of a town near Osaka
大阪城	Osaka Castle, a famous castle in Osaka

II. Translation

Sentence Patterns
1. I [am going to] go to Kyoto.
2. I [am going to] go home by taxi.
3. I came to Japan with my family.

Example Sentences
1. Where are you going tomorrow?
   ……[I'm going] to Nara.

2. Where did you go on Sunday?
   ……I didn't go anywhere.

3. How are you getting to Tokyo?
   ……[I'm going] on the bullet train.

4. Who are you going to Tokyo with?
   ……[I'm going with] Mr. Yamada.

5. When did you arrive in Japan?
   ……[I arrived] on the twenty-fifth of March.

6. When's your birthday?
   ……[It's on] the thirteenth of June.

Conversation

Does this train go to Koshien?

Santos:	Excuse me. How much is it to Koshien?
Woman:	It's 350 yen.
Santos:	350 yen? Thank you.
Woman:	You're welcome.
	……………………………………………………
Santos:	Excuse me, which platform for Koshien, please?
Station attendant:	Number 5.
Santos:	Thanks.
	……………………………………………………
Santos:	Excuse me, does this train go to Koshien?
Man:	No, the next local train does.
Santos:	Oh, I see. Thanks.

III. Useful Words and Information

祝祭日　**National Holidays**

がつついたち 1月1日	がんじつ 元日	New Year's Day
がつだい　げつようび 1月第2月曜日**	せいじん　ひ 成人の日	Coming-of-Age Day
がつ　にち 2月11日	けんこくきねん　ひ 建国記念の日	National Foundation Day
がつ　はつか 3月20日*	しゅんぶん　ひ 春分の日	Vernal Equinox Day
がつ　にち 4月29日	しょうわ　ひ 昭和の日	Showa Day
がつみっか 5月3日	けんぽうきねんび 憲法記念日	Constitution Memorial Day
がつよっか 5月4日	ひ みどりの日	Greenery Day
がついつか 5月5日	ひ こどもの日	Children's Day
がつだい　げつようび 7月第3月曜日***	うみ　ひ 海の日	Marine Day
がつだい　げつようび 9月第3月曜日***	けいろう　ひ 敬老の日	Respect-for-the-Aged Day
がつ　にち 9月23日*	しゅうぶん　ひ 秋分の日	Autumnal Equinox Day
がつだい　げつようび 10月第2月曜日**	たいいく　ひ 体育の日	Health and Sports Day
がつみっか 11月3日	ぶんか　ひ 文化の日	Culture Day
がつ　にち 11月23日	きんろうかんしゃ　ひ 勤労感謝の日	Labour Thanksgiving Day
がつ　にち 12月23日	てんのうたんじょうび 天皇誕生日	The Emperor's Birthday

* Varies from year to year.

** The second Monday

*** The third Monday

 If a national holiday falls on a Sunday, the following Monday is taken off instead.
The week from 29th April to 5th May, which contains a series of holidays, is called ゴールデンウィーク (Golden Week). Some companies make the whole of this week a holiday for their employees.

IV. Grammar Notes

1. $\boxed{\text{N(place)} \land \text{行きます／来ます／帰ります}}$

When a verb indicates movement to a certain place, the particle へ is put after the place noun to show the direction of the move.

① 京都へ 行きます。   I'm going to Kyoto.

② 日本へ 来ました。   I came to Japan.

③ うちへ 帰ります。   I'm going home.

[Note] The particle へ is read え.

2. $\boxed{\text{どこ[へ]も 行きません／行きませんでした}}$

When you want to deny everything covered by an interrogative, you attach the particle も to the interrogative and put the verb in its negative form.

④ どこ[へ]も 行きません。   I'm not going anywhere.

⑤ 何も 食べません。   I'm not going to eat anything. (See Lesson 6.)

⑥ だれも 来ませんでした。   Nobody came.

3. $\boxed{\text{N(vehicle)で 行きます／来ます／帰ります}}$

The particle で indicates a means or method. The speaker attaches it after a noun representing a vehicle and uses it together with a movement verb to indicate his or her means of transport.

⑦ 電車で 行きます。   I'm going by train.

⑧ タクシーで 来ました。   I came by taxi.

When talking about walking somewhere, the speaker uses the expression あるいて. In this case, the particle で is not used.

⑨ 駅から 歩いて 帰りました。   I walked home from the station.

4. $\boxed{\text{N(person/animal)と V}}$

When talking about doing something with a person or an animal, the person or animal is marked with the particle と.

⑩ 家族と 日本へ 来ました。   I came to Japan with my family.

If doing something by oneself, the expression ひとりで is used. In this case, the particle と is not used.

⑪ 一人で 東京へ 行きます。   I'm going to Tokyo on my own.

5. いつ

To ask about time, interrogatives using なん, such as なんじ, なんようび and なんがつなんにち are used. The interrogative いつ (when) is also used to ask when something will happen or happened. いつ does not take the particle に.

⑫ いつ 日本へ 来ましたか。
　　……3月 25日に 来ました。

When did you come to Japan?
……[I came] on 25th March.

⑬ いつ 広島へ 行きますか。
　　……来週 行きます。

When are you going to Hiroshima?
……[I'm going] next week.

6. ～よ

The particle よ is placed at the end of a sentence. It is used to emphasise information which the listener does not know, or to show that the speaker is giving his or her judgement or views assertively.

⑭ この 電車は 甲子園へ 行きますか。
　　……いいえ、行きません。次の「普通」ですよ。

Does this train go to Koshien?
……No, it doesn't. You need the next local train.

⑮ 北海道に 馬が たくさん いますよ。

There are a lot of horses in Hokkaido, you know. (See Lesson 18.)

⑯ マリアさん、この アイスクリーム、おいしいですよ。

Maria, this ice cream is very nice, you know. (See Lesson 19.)

7. そうですね

The expression そうですね is used to express sympathy or agreement with what the speaker has said. It is similar to the expression そうですか (see Lesson 2-8), but while そうですか is used by a speaker to acknowledge the receipt of some new information, そうですね is used to show sympathy or agreement with something the speaker already thought or knew.

⑰ あしたは 日曜日ですね。
　　……あ、そうですね。

It's Sunday tomorrow, isn't it?
……Oh, yes, so it is.

5

39

Lesson 6

I. Vocabulary

たべます	食べます	eat
のみます	飲みます	drink
すいます［たばこを〜］	吸います	smoke [a cigarette]
みます	見ます	see, look at, watch
ききます	聞きます	hear, listen
よみます	読みます	read
かきます	書きます	write (かきます can also mean to draw or paint, but in this case it is written with hiragana in this book)
かいます	買います	buy
とります 　［しゃしんを〜］	撮ります 　［写真を〜］	take [a photograph]
します		do, play
あいます 　［ともだちに〜］	会います［友達に〜］	meet [a friend]
ごはん		a meal, cooked rice
あさごはん*	朝ごはん	breakfast
ひるごはん	昼ごはん	lunch
ばんごはん*	晩ごはん	supper
パン		bread
たまご	卵	egg
にく	肉	meat
さかな	魚	fish
やさい	野菜	vegetable
くだもの	果物	fruit
みず	水	water
おちゃ	お茶	tea, green tea
こうちゃ	紅茶	black tea
ぎゅうにゅう（ミルク）	牛乳	milk
ジュース		juice
ビール		beer
［お］さけ	［お］酒	alcohol, Japanese rice wine
たばこ		tobacco, cigarette

てがみ	手紙	letter
レポート		report
しゃしん	写真	photograph
ビデオ		video [tape], video deck
みせ	店	shop, store
にわ	庭	garden
しゅくだい	宿題	homework（～を します：do homework）
テニス		tennis（～を します：play tennis）
サッカー		soccer, football（～を します：play soccer）
[お]はなみ	[お]花見	cherry-blossom viewing（～を します：view the cherry blossoms）
なに	何	what
いっしょに		together
ちょっと		a little while, a little bit
いつも		always, usually
ときどき	時々	sometimes
それから		after that, and then
ええ		yes
いいですね。		That's good.
わかりました。		I see.

〈会話〉

何ですか。	Yes?（lit: What is it?）
じゃ、また [あした]。	See you [tomorrow].

....

メキシコ	Mexico
大阪デパート	a fictitious department store
つるや	a fictitious restaurant
フランス屋	a fictitious supermarket
毎日屋	a fictitious supermarket

II. Translation

Sentence Patterns
1. I [am going to] read a book.
2. I [am going to] buy a newspaper at the station.
3. Shall we go to Kobe together?
4. Let's take a bit of a break.

Example Sentences
1. Do you drink alcohol?
   ······No, I don't.

2. What do you usually have to eat in the morning?
   ······I have bread and eggs.

3. What did you have to eat this morning?
   ······I didn't have anything.

4. What did you do on Saturday?
   ······I studied Japanese, then I watched a film with some friends.

5. Where did you buy that bag?
   ······[I bought it] in Mexico.

6. Shall we play tennis tomorrow?
   ······Yes, that would be great.

7. Let's meet at the station tomorrow at ten o'clock.
   ······OK.

Conversation

Shall we go together?

Sato: Mr. Miller!

Miller: Yes?

Sato: I'm going to see the cherry blossoms tomorrow with some friends. Would you like to come with us, Mr. Miller?

Miller: That sounds good. Where are you going?

Sato: Osaka Castle.

Miller: What time shall we go?

Sato: Let's meet at Osaka Station at ten o'clock.

Miller: OK.

Sato: See you tomorrow, then.

III. Useful Words and Information

食べ物　Food

野菜　Vegetables

きゅうり	cucumber
トマト	tomato
なす	aubergine, eggplant
まめ	beans, peas
キャベツ	cabbage
ねぎ	spring onion, scallion
はくさい	Chinese cabbage
ほうれんそう	spinach
レタス	lettuce
じゃがいも	potato
だいこん	Japanese radish, mooli
たまねぎ	onion
にんじん	carrot

果物　Fruit

いちご	strawberry	かき	persimmon
もも	peach	みかん	mandarin orange
すいか	watermelon	りんご	apple
ぶどう	grape	バナナ	banana
なし	Japanese pear		

肉　Meat

ぎゅうにく	beef
とりにく	chicken
ぶたにく	pork
ソーセージ	sausage
ハム	ham

こめ　rice

たまご　egg

魚　Fish

あじ	horse mackerel	さけ	salmon	えび	lobster, shrimp
いわし	sardine	まぐろ	tuna	かに	crab
さば	mackerel	たい	sea bream	いか	cuttlefish, squid
さんま	mackerel pike	たら	cod	たこ	octopus

かい　shellfish

 Japan depends on imports for more than half of its food. Its food self-sufficiency rates are as follows: cereals 59%, vegetables 81%, fruit 38%, meat 56%, and seafood 60% (2010, Ministry of Agriculture, Forestry, and Fisheries). The self-sufficiency rate of rice (the country's staple food) is 100%.

6

43

IV. Grammar Notes

1. | N を V(transitive) |

The particle を is used to indicate the direct object of a transitive verb.

① ジュースを 飲みます。　　　I drink juice.

[Note] を is used only in writing the particle.

2. | N を します |

A fairly wide range of nouns are used as the objects of the verb します, which means that the action denoted by the noun is performed. Some examples are shown below.

1) Play sports or games

　　　サッカーを します　play soccer　　トランプを します　play cards

2) Hold gatherings or events

　　　パーティーを します　give a party　　会議を します　hold a meeting

3) Do something

　　　宿題を します　do homework　　仕事を します　work
　　　電話を します　call, phone

3. | 何を しますか |

This is a question to ask about someone's actions.

② 月曜日 何を しますか。　　　What are you doing on Monday?
　……京都へ 行きます。　　　……I'm going to Kyoto.

③ きのう 何を しましたか。　　What did you do yesterday?
　……サッカーを しました。　　……I played soccer.

4. | なん and なに |

Both なん and なに mean 'what'.

なん is used in the following cases:

1) When it precedes a word whose first sound is in the た, だ or な -row.

④ それは 何ですか。　　　　What's that?

⑤ 何の 本ですか。　　　　　What's that book about?

⑥ 寝る まえに、何と 言いますか。

　　What do you say before going to bed? (See Lesson 21.)

⑦ 何で 東京へ 行きますか。　How are you getting to Tokyo?

[Note] なんで is used for asking 'Why?' as well as 'How?' なにで can be used when the speaker wants to make it clear that he or she is asking 'How?'

⑧ 何で 東京へ 行きますか。　How are you getting to Tokyo?
　……新幹線で 行きます。　　……I'm going on the Shinkansen.

2) When using it with a counter suffix.

⑨ テレーザちゃんは 何歳ですか。　　How old is Teresa?

なに is used in all other cases apart from 1) and 2).

⑩ 何を 買いますか。　　What are you going to buy?

5. ［ N（place）で V ］

When added after a noun denoting a place, the particle で indicates the occurrence of an action in that place.

⑪ 駅で 新聞を 買います。　　I'm going to buy a paper at the station.

6. ［ V ませんか ］

This expression is used when the speaker wants to invite someone to do something.

⑫ いっしょに 京都へ 行きませんか。　Would you like to come to Kyoto with us?
　……ええ、いいですね。　　　　……Yes, that's a nice idea.

7. ［ V ましょう ］

This expression is used when a speaker is positively inviting the listener to do something with the speaker. It is also used when responding positively to an invitation.

⑬ ちょっと 休みましょう。　　Let's take a break.
⑭ いっしょに 昼ごはんを 食べませんか。　Shall we have lunch together?
　……ええ、食べましょう。　　……Yes, let's do that.

[Note] V ませんか and V ましょう are both used to invite someone to do something, but V ませんか shows that the speaker is giving more consideration to what the listener might want than V ましょう.

8. ［ 〜か ］

か indicates that the listener has received and accepted some new information. It is used in the same way as the か in そうですか（see Lesson 2-8）.

⑮ 日曜日 京都へ 行きました。　　I went to Kyoto on Sunday.
　……京都ですか。いいですね。　　……Kyoto, eh? Great!

Lesson 7

I. Vocabulary

きります	切ります	cut, slice
おくります	送ります	send
あげます		give
もらいます		receive
かします	貸します	lend
かります	借ります	borrow
おしえます	教えます	teach
ならいます	習います	learn
かけます [でんわを～]	[電話を～]	make [a telephone call]
て	手	hand, arm
はし		chopsticks
スプーン		spoon
ナイフ		knife
フォーク		fork
はさみ		scissors
パソコン		personal computer
ケータイ		mobile phone, cell phone
メール		e-mail
ねんがじょう	年賀状	New Year's greeting card
パンチ		punch
ホッチキス		stapler
セロテープ		Sellotape, Scotch tape, clear adhesive tape
けしゴム	消しゴム	rubber, eraser
かみ	紙	paper
はな	花	flower, blossom
シャツ		shirt
プレゼント		present, gift
にもつ	荷物	luggage, baggage, parcel
おかね	お金	money
きっぷ	切符	ticket
クリスマス		Christmas

ちち	父	(my) father
はは	母	(my) mother
おとうさん*	お父さん	(someone else's) father (also used to address one's own father)
おかあさん	お母さん	(someone else's) mother (also used to address one's own mother)
もう		already
まだ		not yet
これから		from now on, soon

〈練習 C〉

[～、] すてきですね。 — What a nice [～]!

〈会話〉

いらっしゃい。	How nice of you to come. (lit. Welcome.)
どうぞ お上がり ください。	Do come in.
失礼します。	May I? (lit. I commit an incivility.)
[～は] いかがですか。	Won't you have [～]?/Would you like to have [～]? (used when offering something)
いただきます。	Thank you./I accept. (said before starting to eat or drink)
ごちそうさま[でした]*。	That was delicious. (said after eating or drinking)

....

スペイン	Spain

II. Translation

Sentence Patterns

1. I [am going to] watch a film on my PC.
2. I [am going to] give some flowers to Ms. Kimura.
3. Karina gave me some chocolates (lit. I received some chocolates from Karina.)
4. I've already sent an e-mail.

Example Sentences

1. Did you study Japanese on the TV?
   ······No, I studied it on the radio.

2. Do you write your reports in Japanese?
   ······No, I write them in English.

3. What's 'Goodbye' in Japanese?
   ······It's 'Sayonara'.

4. Who do you write New Year's cards to?
   ······I write them to my teachers and friends.

5. What's that?
   ······It's a personal organiser. Mr. Yamada gave it to me.

6. Have you bought the tickets for the bullet train yet?
   ······Yes, I have [already bought them].

7. Have you had lunch yet?
   ······No, not yet. I'm just about to.

Conversation

Welcome

Ichiro Yamada:	Yes?
Jose Santos:	It's Jose Santos.

....

Ichiro Yamada:	Hello. (lit:Welcome.) Please come in.
Jose Santos:	Thank you.

....

Tomoko Yamada:	Would you like some coffee?
Maria Santos:	Yes, please.

....

Tomoko Yamada:	Here you are.
Maria Santos:	Thank you.
	This is a lovely spoon, isn't it?
Tomoko Yamada:	Yes, I was given it by someone at work.
	It's a souvenir from Mexico.

III. Useful Words and Information

家族　　Family

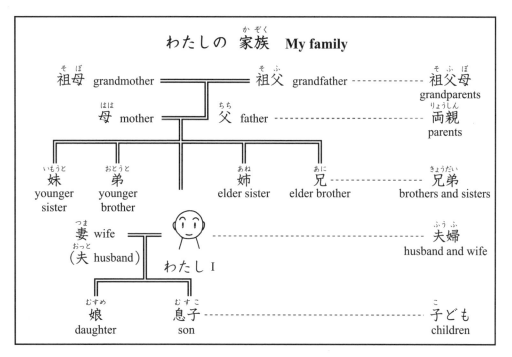

わたしの　家族　My family

祖母 grandmother ━━━━━ 祖父 grandfather ------------ 祖父母 grandparents

母 mother ━━━━━ 父 father ---------------------- 両親 parents

妹 younger sister　弟 younger brother　姉 elder sister　兄 elder brother ------- 兄弟 brothers and sisters

妻 wife
（夫 husband）
わたし I ----------- 夫婦 husband and wife

娘 daughter　息子 son ------------------- 子ども children

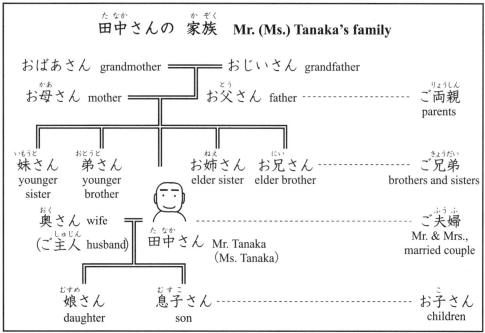

田中さんの　家族　Mr. (Ms.) Tanaka's family

おばあさん grandmother ━━━━━ おじいさん grandfather

お母さん mother ━━━━━ お父さん father ----------------- ご両親 parents

妹さん younger sister　弟さん younger brother　お姉さん elder sister　お兄さん elder brother ------------- ご兄弟 brothers and sisters

奥さん wife
（ご主人 husband）
田中さん Mr. Tanaka（Ms. Tanaka） ----------- ご夫婦 Mr. & Mrs., married couple

娘さん daughter　息子さん son ------------------- お子さん children

IV. Grammar Notes

1. | N（tool/means）で V |

The particle で indicates a method or means used for an action.

① はしで 食べます。 I eat with chopsticks.

② 日本語で レポートを 書きます。 I'm going to write the report in Japanese.

2. | 'Word/Sentence' は ～語で 何ですか |

This question is used to ask how to say a word or sentence in another language.

③ 「ありがとう」は 英語で 何ですか。 What's 'Arigato' in English?
…… 「Thank you」です。 ……It's 'thank you'.

④ 「Thank you」は 日本語で 何ですか。 What's 'thank you' in Japanese?
…… 「ありがとう」です。 ……It's 'Arigato'.

3. | N₁（person）に N₂を あげます, etc. |

Verbs like あげます, かします and おしえます indicate imparting things or information, so they must be used with a noun saying to whom those things or information are imparted. The particle に is used to denote the recipient.

⑤ ［わたしは］木村さんに 花を あげました。 I gave Ms. Kimura some flowers.

⑥ ［わたしは］イーさんに 本を 貸しました。 I lent Ms. Lee a book.

⑦ ［わたしは］山田さんに 英語を 教えます。 I teach Mr. Yamada English.

4. | N₁（person）に N₂を もらいます, etc. |

Verbs like もらいます, かります and ならいます indicate receiving things or information, so they are used with a noun indicating the person from whom those things or information are received. The particle に is used to denote that person.

⑧ ［わたしは］山田さんに 花を もらいました。
I received some flowers from Mr. Yamada.

⑨ ［わたしは］カリナさんに CDを 借りました。
I borrowed a CD from Karina.

⑩ ［わたしは］ワンさんに 中国語を 習います。
I'm learning Chinese from Mr. Wang.

[Note] から can be used instead of に in this sentence pattern. から is always used when receiving something from an organisation such as a company or school rather than a person.

⑪ ［わたしは］山田さんから 花を もらいました。
I received some flowers from Mr. Yamada.

⑫ 銀行から お金を 借りました。
I borrowed some money from the bank.

5. もう V ました

もう means 'already' and is used with V ました. In this case, V ました means that the action has been completed.

The answer to the question もう V ましたか as to whether an action has been completed or not is はい、もう V ました if in the affirmative (i.e. the action has been completed) and いいえ、V て いません (see Lesson 31) or いいえ、まだです if in the negative (i.e. the action has not been completed). いいえ、V ませんでした is not used in this case, since this means that something was not done in the past, rather than that something has not been completed in the present.

⑬ もう 荷物を 送りましたか。   Have you sent the baggage yet?

   ……はい、[もう] 送りました。   ……Yes, I have [sent it].

   ……いいえ、まだ 送って いません。   ……No, I haven't sent it yet.

                                      (See Lesson 31.)

   ……いいえ、まだです。   ……No, not yet.

6. Omission of particles

Particles are often omitted in informal speech when the relationships between the parts of speech before and after them are obvious.

⑭ この スプーン[は]、すてきですね。   This is a lovely spoon, isn't it?

⑮ コーヒー[を]、もう 一杯 いかがですか。

Would you like another cup of coffee? (See Lesson 8.)

7

51

Lesson 8

I. Vocabulary

ハンサム[な]		handsome
きれい[な]		beautiful, clean
しずか[な]	静か[な]	quiet
にぎやか[な]		lively
ゆうめい[な]	有名[な]	famous
しんせつ[な]	親切[な]	helpful, kind, considerate（not used about one's own family members)
げんき[な]	元気[な]	healthy, energetic, cheerful
ひま[な]	暇[な]	free（time)
べんり[な]	便利[な]	convenient
すてき[な]		fine, nice, wonderful
おおきい	大きい	big, large
ちいさい*	小さい	small, little
あたらしい	新しい	new, fresh
ふるい	古い	old（not used to describe a person's age)
いい（よい）		good
わるい*	悪い	bad
あつい	暑い、熱い	hot
さむい	寒い	cold（referring to temperature)
つめたい	冷たい	cold（referring to touch)
むずかしい	難しい	difficult
やさしい	易しい	easy
たかい	高い	expensive, tall, high
やすい	安い	inexpensive, cheap
ひくい*	低い	low
おもしろい		interesting
おいしい		delicious, tasty
いそがしい	忙しい	busy
たのしい	楽しい	enjoyable
しろい	白い	white
くろい	黒い	black
あかい	赤い	red
あおい	青い	blue
さくら	桜	cherry（blossom)
やま	山	mountain
まち	町	town, city
たべもの	食べ物	food

ところ	所	place
りょう	寮	dormitory
レストラン		restaurant
せいかつ	生活	life
[お]しごと	[お]仕事	work, business （〜を します：do one's job, work）
どう		how
どんな 〜		what kind of 〜
とても		very
あまり		not so （used with negatives）
そして		and （used to connect sentences）
〜が、〜		〜, but 〜

〈練習 C〉

| お元気ですか。 | How are you? |
| そうですね。 | Well let me see. （pausing） |

〈会話〉

[〜、] もう 一杯 いかがですか。	Won't you have another cup of [〜]?
[いいえ、] けっこうです。	No, thank you.
もう 〜です[ね]。	It's already 〜[, isn't it?]
そろそろ 失礼します。	It's time I was going.
いいえ。	Not at all.
また いらっしゃって ください。	Please come again.

シャンハイ	Shanghai （上海）
金閣寺	Kinkakuji Temple （the Golden Pavilion）
奈良公園	Nara Park
富士山	Mt. Fuji, the highest mountain in Japan
「七人の 侍」	'The Seven Samurai', a classic movie by Akira Kurosawa

II. Translation

Sentence Patterns

1. Cherry blossoms are beautiful.
2. Mt. Fuji is high.
3. Cherry blossoms are beautiful flowers.
4. Mt. Fuji is a high mountain.

Example Sentences

1. Is Osaka lively?
   ⋯⋯Yes, it is [lively].

2. Is Sakura University well-known?
   ⋯⋯No, it's not [well-known].

3. Is it cold in Beijing at the moment?
   ⋯⋯Yes, it's very cold.

   Is it cold in Shanghai too?
   ⋯⋯No, it isn't [very cold].

4. How's the university dormitory?
   ⋯⋯It's old, but it's convenient.

5. I went to Mr. Matsumoto's house yesterday.
   ⋯⋯What's his house like?
   It's a beautiful house, and it's [a] big [house].

6. I watched an interesting film yesterday.
   ⋯⋯What did you watch?
   'The Seven Samurai'.

Conversation

It's time we were going

Ichiro Yamada:	Maria, how do you find living in Japan?
Maria Santos:	Every day is great fun.
Ichiro Yamada:	Really? Mr. Santos, how's your work going?
Jose Santos:	Well, it's busy, but it's interesting.
	⋯⋯⋯⋯⋯⋯⋯⋯⋯⋯⋯⋯⋯⋯⋯⋯⋯⋯⋯⋯
Tomoko Yamada:	Would you like another cup of coffee?
Maria Santos:	No, I'm fine, thank you.
	⋯⋯⋯⋯⋯⋯⋯⋯⋯⋯⋯⋯⋯⋯⋯⋯⋯⋯⋯⋯
Jose Santos:	Oh, it's already six o'clock, isn't it? It's time we were going.
Ichiro Yamada:	Really?
Maria Santos:	Thank you very much for today.
Tomoko Yamada:	Not at all. Please come again.

III. Useful Words and Information

色・味　Colours and Tastes

色 Colours

	noun	adjective		noun	adjective
白	white	白い	黄色	yellow	黄色い
黒	black	黒い	茶色	brown	茶色い
赤	red	赤い	ピンク	pink	—
青	blue	青い	オレンジ	orange	—
緑	green	—	グレー	gray	—
紫	purple	—	ベージュ	beige	—

8

味 Tastes

 甘い sweet　　 辛い hot (spicy)　　 苦い bitter　　 塩辛い salty

 酸っぱい sour　　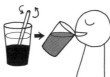 濃い strong　　 薄い weak

55

 春・夏・秋・冬 **Spring, Summer, Autumn, Winter**

The four seasons are clearly defined in Japan. Spring is from March to May, summer from June to August, autumn from September to November, and winter from December to February. The average temperature varies from place to place, but the pattern of change is almost the same (see graph). August is the hottest month, and January or February are the coldest. As a result of these temperature changes, Japanese people feel that spring is warm, summer hot, autumn cool, and winter cold.

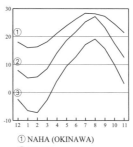

① NAHA (OKINAWA)
② TOKYO
③ ABASHIRI (HOKKAIDO)

IV. Grammar Notes

1. Adjectives

Adjectives are used as predicates, and in sentences like Nは adj です they indicate the state of a noun or are used to modify a noun. They are divided into one of two groups, い -adjectives and な -adjectives, depending on how they inflect.

2.

> N は な -adj[な]です
> N は い -adj(〜い)です

Adjective sentences that are non-past and affirmative end in です, which shows politeness toward the listener. Both types of adjective are attached to the front of です, but な -adjectives drop their な, while い -adjectives retain their (〜い).

① ワット先生は 親切です。　　　　　　Mr. Watt is kind.

② 富士山は 高いです。　　　　　　　　Mt. Fuji is high.

1) な -adj[な]じゃ(では) ありません

The non-past negative of a な -adj is formed by dropping the な and attaching じゃ(では) ありません to it.

③ あそこは 静かじゃ(では) ありません。　　It's not quiet there.

2) い -adj(〜い)です　→　〜くないです

The non-past negative of an い-adjective is formed by dropping the final い and attaching くないです to it.

④ この 本は おもしろくないです。　　　This book is not interesting.

[Note] The negative of いいです is よくないです.

3) Adjectival Inflections

	な -adjectives	い -adjectives
Non-past affirmative	しんせつです	たかいです
Non-past negative	しんせつじゃ(では) ありません	たかくないです

4) Questions using adjective sentences are formed in the same way as those using noun sentences (see Lesson 1) and verb sentences (see Lesson 4). To answer such a question, the adjective is repeated. Expressions such as そうです or ちがいます cannot be used.

⑤ ペキンは 寒いですか。　　　　　　　Is it cold in Beijing?
　……はい、寒いです。　　　　　　　　……Yes, it is [cold].

⑥ 奈良公園は にぎやかですか。　　　　Is Nara Park busy?
　……いいえ、にぎやかじゃ ありません。　……No, it isn't [busy].

3.

> な -adj な N
> い -adj(〜い) N

When an adjective is used to modify a noun, it is placed in front of the noun. な -adjectives keep their な in this case.

⑦ ワット先生は 親切な 先生です。　　　Mr. Watt is a considerate teacher.

⑧ 富士山は 高い 山です。　　　Mt. Fuji is a high mountain.

4. ～が、～

が connects two statements in an antithetical relationship. When these are adjective clauses with the same subject, if the initial clause remarks on the subject positively, the subsequent clause will remark on it negatively, and vice versa.

⑨ 日本の 食べ物は おいしいですが、高いです。

　　Japanese food is delicious, but it is expensive.

5. とても／あまり

とても and あまり are both adverbs of degree, and both come before the adjectives they modify. とても is used in affirmative sentences, and means 'very'. あまり, used with a negative, means 'not very'.

⑩ ペキンは とても 寒いです。　　　Beijing is very cold.

⑪ これは とても 有名な 映画です。　　　This is a very famous movie.

⑫ シャンハイは あまり 寒くないです。　　　Shanghai is not very cold.

⑬ さくら大学は あまり 有名な 大学じゃ ありません。

　　Sakura University is not a very well-known university.

6. N は どうですか

The question Nは どうですか is used to inquire about the listener's impression, opinion or feelings about a thing, place, person, etc. that he or she has experienced, visited or met.

⑭ 日本の 生活は どうですか。　　　How do you find life in Japan?

　　……楽しいです。　　　……It's fun.

7. N₁ は どんな N₂ ですか

どんな modifies a noun and is an interrogative used for inquiring about the state or nature of a person, thing, etc.

⑮ 奈良は どんな 町ですか。　　　What sort of town is Nara?

　　……古い 町です。　　　……It's an old town.

8. そうですね

The use of the expression そうですね to express agreement or sympathy was explained in Lesson 5. The そうですね that appears in the Conversation of this lesson shows that the speaker is thinking, as in ⑯ below.

⑯ お仕事は どうですか。　　　How's your work going?

　　……そうですね。忙しいですが、おもしろいです。

　　……Well, it's busy, but it's interesting.

8

Lesson 9

I. Vocabulary

わかります		understand
あります		have
すき[な]	好き[な]	like
きらい[な]	嫌い[な]	dislike
じょうず[な]	上手[な]	good at
へた[な]	下手[な]	poor at
のみもの	飲み物	drinks
りょうり	料理	dish (cooked food), cooking (〜を します：cook)
スポーツ		sport (〜を します：play sports)
やきゅう	野球	baseball (〜を します：play baseball)
ダンス		dance (〜を します：dance)
りょこう	旅行	trip, tour (〜[を] します：travel, make a trip)
おんがく	音楽	music
うた	歌	song
クラシック		classical music
ジャズ		jazz
コンサート		concert
カラオケ		karaoke
かぶき	歌舞伎	Kabuki (traditional Japanese musical drama)
え	絵	picture, drawing
じ*	字	letter, character
かんじ	漢字	Chinese character
ひらがな		hiragana script
かたかな		katakana script
ローマじ*	ローマ字	the Roman alphabet
こまかい おかね	細かい お金	small change
チケット		ticket
じかん	時間	time
ようじ	用事	something to do, errand
やくそく	約束	appointment, promise (〜[を] します：promise)

アルバイト		side job (〜を します：work part-time)
ごしゅじん	ご主人	(someone else's) husband
おっと／しゅじん	夫／主人	(my) husband
おくさん	奥さん	(someone else's) wife
つま／かない	妻／家内	(my) wife
こども	子ども	child
よく		well, much
だいたい		mostly, roughly
たくさん		many, much
すこし	少し	a little, a few
ぜんぜん	全然	not at all (used with negatives)
はやく	早く、速く	early, quickly, fast
〜から		because 〜
どうして		why

〈練習 C〉

貸して ください。	Please lend (it to me).
いいですよ。	Sure./Certainly.
残念です［が］	I'm sorry [, but], unfortunately

〈会話〉

ああ	oh
いっしょに いかがですか。	Won't you join me (us)?
［〜は］ちょっと……。	[〜] is a bit difficult. (a euphemism used when declining an invitation)
だめですか。	So you can't (come)?
また 今度 お願いします。	Please ask me again some other time. (used when refusing an invitation indirectly, considering someone's feelings)

II. Translation

Sentence Patterns

1. I like Italian food.
2. I can understand a bit of Japanese.
3. It's my son's (daughter's) birthday today, so I'm going home early.

Example Sentences

1. Do you like alcohol?
   ……No, I don't [like it].

2. What sports do you like?
   ……I like soccer.

3. Is Karina good at painting?
   ……Yes, she's very good.

4. Do you understand Indonesian, Ms. Tanaka?
   ……No, not at all.

5. Do you have any small change?
   ……No, I don't.

6. Do you read the newspaper every morning?
   ……No, I don't; I don't have time.

7. Why did you go home early yesterday?
   ……Because there was something I had to do.

Conversation

It's a pity……

Kimura: Yes?

Miller: Is that Ms. Kimura? This is Mike Miller.

Kimura: Oh, Mr. Miller. Good evening. Are you well?

Miller: Yes, I'm fine.
          Umm…… Ms. Kimura, would you like to come to a classical concert with me?

Kimura: That sounds nice. When is it?

Miller: Next week, on Friday evening.

Kimura: Friday?
          Friday evening's not so good for me.

Miller: So you can't come?

Kimura: No, it's a pity, but I've arranged to meet some friends……

Miller: I see.

Kimura: Yes. Please ask me another time.

III. Useful Words and Information

音楽・スポーツ・映画　　Music, Sports and Films

音楽 Music

ポップス	pop
ロック	rock
ジャズ	jazz
ラテン	Latin-American
クラシック	classical
民謡	folk
演歌	traditional Japanese popular songs
ミュージカル	musical
オペラ	opera

映画 Films

SF	science fiction
ホラー	horror
アニメ	cartoon
ドキュメンタリー	documentary
恋愛	romance
ミステリー	mystery
文芸	film based on a classic work
戦争	war
アクション	action
喜劇	comedy

スポーツ Sports

ソフトボール	softball	野球	baseball
サッカー	soccer	卓球／ピンポン	table tennis, ping-pong
ラグビー	rugby	相撲	sumo
バレーボール	volleyball	柔道	judo
バスケットボール	basketball	剣道	Japanese fencing
テニス	tennis	水泳	swimming
ボウリング	bowling		
スキー	skiing		
スケート	skating		

IV. Grammar Notes

1.
> N が あります／わかります
> N が 好^すきです／嫌^{きら}いです／上手^{じょうず}です／下手^{へた}です

The objects of some verbs and adjectives are marked with が.

① わたしは イタリア料理^{りょうり}が 好^すきです。　　I like Italian food.

② わたしは 日本語^{にほんご}が わかります。　　I understand Japanese.

③ わたしは 車^{くるま}が あります。　　I have a car.

2.
> どんな N

In addition to the responses explained in Lesson 8, a question sentence using どんな may be replied to by stating a specific name.

④ どんな スポーツが 好^すきですか。　　What sports do you like?
　　……サッカーが 好^すきです。　　……I like soccer.

3.
> よく／だいたい／たくさん／少^{すこ}し／あまり／全然^{ぜんぜん}

These adverbs are placed before verbs to modify them.

	Adverbs of degree	Adverbs of quantity
Used with an affirmative	よく　　わかります だいたい わかります すこし　　わかります	たくさん あります すこし　　あります
Used with a negative	あまり　　わかりません ぜんぜん わかりません	あまり　　ありません ぜんぜん ありません

⑤ 英語^{えいご}が よく わかります。　　I understand English well.

⑥ 英語^{えいご}が 少^{すこ}し わかります。　　I understand English a little.

⑦ 英語^{えいご}が あまり わかりません。　　I don't understand English very well.

⑧ お金^{かね}が たくさん あります。　　I have a lot of money.

⑨ お金^{かね}が 全然^{ぜんぜん} ありません。　　I don't have any money.

[Note]すこし, ぜんぜん and あまり can also modify adjectives.

⑩ ここは 少^{すこ}し 寒^{さむ}いです。　　It's a little cold here.

⑪ あの 映画^{えいが}は 全然^{ぜんぜん} おもしろくないです。

　　That film is not at all interesting.

4. 〜から、〜

A statement before から gives the reason for a statement after it.

⑫ 時間が ありませんから、新聞を 読みません。

I don't read newspapers because I don't have time.

It is also possible to state something and add the reason after it by adding 〜から.

⑬ 毎朝 新聞を 読みますか。
……いいえ、読みません。時間が ありませんから。

Do you read a newspaper every morning?
……No, I don't. I don't have time.

5. どうして

The interrogative どうして is used to ask the reason for something. から is placed at the end of the reply giving the reason.

⑭ どうして 朝 新聞を 読みませんか。
……時間が ありませんから。

Why don't you read a newspaper in the mornings?
……Because I don't have time.

The question どうしてですか is used to ask the reason for something the other person has just said, instead of repeating what they said.

⑮ きょうは 早く 帰ります。　　I'm going home early today.
　　……どうしてですか。　　　 ……Why?
　　子どもの 誕生日ですから。　Because it's my son's (daughter's) birthday.

Lesson 10

I. Vocabulary

あります		exist, be〔referring to inanimate things〕
います		exist, be〔referring to animate things〕
いろいろ［な］		various
おとこの ひと	男の 人	man
おんなの ひと	女の 人	woman
おとこの こ	男の 子	boy
おんなの こ	女の 子	girl
いぬ	犬	dog
ねこ	猫	cat
パンダ		panda
ぞう	象	elephant
き	木	tree, wood
もの	物	thing
でんち	電池	battery
はこ	箱	box
スイッチ		switch
れいぞうこ	冷蔵庫	refrigerator
テーブル		table
ベッド		bed
たな	棚	shelf
ドア		door
まど	窓	window
ポスト		postbox, mailbox
ビル		building
ATM		cash machine, ATM〔Automatic Teller Machine〕
コンビニ		convenience store
こうえん	公園	park
きっさてん	喫茶店	café, coffee shop
～や	～屋	～ shop, ～ store
のりば	乗り場	a fixed place to catch taxis, trains, etc.
けん	県	prefecture

うえ	上	on, above, over
した	下	under, below, beneath
まえ	前	front, before
うしろ		back, behind
みぎ	右	right [side]
ひだり	左	left [side]
なか	中	in, inside
そと*	外	outside
となり	隣	next, next door
ちかく	近く	near, vicinity
あいだ	間	between, among

| 〜や 〜［など］ | | 〜, 〜, and so on |

〈会話〉

［どうも］すみません。	Thank you.
ナンプラー	nam pla
コーナー	corner, section
いちばん 下	the bottom

| 東京 ディズニーランド | Tokyo Disneyland |
| アジアストア | a fictitious supermarket |

II. Translation

Sentence Patterns
1. There's a convenience store over there.
2. Ms. Sato's in the lobby.
3. Tokyo Disneyland's in Chiba prefecture.
4. My family's in New York.

Example Sentences
1. Is there a cash machine in this building?
   ······Yes, it's on the second floor.

2. You see that man over there? Who is he?
   ······That's Mr. Matsumoto from IMC.

3. Who's in the garden?
   ······Nobody. There's a cat there.

4. What's in the box?
   ······Some old letters, photographs and other stuff.

5. Where's the post office?
   ······It's near the station, in front of the bank.

6. Where's Mr. Miller?
   ······He's in the meeting room.

Conversation
Do you have any nam pla?

Miller:	Excuse me, where's Asia Store?
Woman:	Asia Store?
	You see that white building over there?
	It's in that building.
Miller:	I see. Thank you.
Woman:	Not at all.

··

Miller:	Excuse me, do you have any nam pla?
Shop Assistant:	Yes.
	There's a Thai food section over there.
	The nam pla's right at the bottom.
Miller:	I see. Thanks.

III. Useful Words and Information

うちの 中 **Inside the House**

① 玄関	entrance hall		⑥ 食堂	dining room	
② トイレ	toilet		⑦ 居間	living room	
③ ふろ場	bathroom		⑧ 寝室	bedroom	
④ 洗面所	washroom		⑨ 廊下	hall	
⑤ 台所	kitchen		⑩ ベランダ	balcony	

10

67

 How to Use a Japanese Bath

① Wash and rinse yourself in the tiled area before getting into the bath.

② Soap and shampoo should never be used in the bath. The bath is for warming yourself and relaxing.

③ When you go out of the bathroom, leave the bath full of hot water and cover it so it stays hot for the next person.

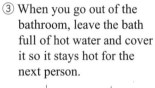

How to Use the Toilet

Japanese-style   Western-style

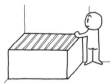

IV. Grammar Notes

1. ┃ N が あります／います ┃

あります and います indicate the existence of a thing, person, etc. Since a sentence using these simply tells the listener that a thing or person exists, the noun representing that thing or person is marked by が.

1) あります is used when what is present is inanimate and cannot move by itself, such as plants and objects.

①	コンピューターが あります。	There's a computer.
②	桜が あります。	There are cherry trees.
③	公園が あります。	There's a park.

2) います is used when what is present is animate and can move by itself, like people and animals.

④	男の 人が います。	There's a man.
⑤	犬が います。	There's a dog.

2. ┃ Place に N が あります／います ┃

This sentence form is used to say what or who is in a certain place.

1) The particle に is used to mark the place where the thing or person is.

⑥	わたしの 部屋に 机が あります。	There's a desk in my room.
⑦	事務所に ミラーさんが います。	Mr. Miller is in the office.

2) The interrogative なに is used when asking what is present, while the interrogative だれ is used when asking who is present.

⑧	地下に 何が ありますか。	What's in the basement?
	……レストランが あります。	……There's a restaurant.
⑨	受付に だれが いますか。	Who's at the reception desk?
	……木村さんが います。	……Ms. Kimura is.

[Note] Remember that the particle used after an interrogative is always が (×なには ×だれは).

3. ┃ N は place に あります／います ┃

This type of sentence takes the noun (the thing that exists) of 2. Place に N が あります／います as its topic and talks about its existence. The noun is positioned at the head of the sentence and is marked with は. In this case, the noun must be something that both the speaker and the listener are aware of.

⑩	東京ディズニーランドは 千葉県に あります。	
	Tokyo Disneyland is in Chiba prefecture.	
⑪	ミラーさんは 事務所に います。	Mr. Miller is in the office.
⑫	東京ディズニーランドは どこに ありますか。	Where's Tokyo Disneyland?

……千葉県に あります。　　　　　　……It's in Chiba prefecture.

⑬　ミラーさんは どこに いますか。　　Where's Mr Miller?
　　……事務所に います。　　　　　　……He's in the office.

[Note] This sentence form can be replaced with N は place です (see Lesson 3).
Note that the interrogative （どこ） or N （ちばけん） which comes before です and
represents the place is not marked by に in this case.

⑭　東京 ディズニーランドは どこですか。　Where's Tokyo Disneyland?
　　……千葉県です。　　　　　　　　　……It's in Chiba prefecture.

4. | N₁（thing/person/place）の N₂（position）|

When the noun N₂ represents a direction or a position, e.g. うえ, した, まえ, うし
ろ, みぎ, ひだり, なか, そと, となり, ちかく or あいだ, it shows a positional
relationship with N₁.

⑮　机の 上に 写真が あります。　　　There's a photograph on the desk.
⑯　郵便局は 銀行の 隣に あります。　The post office is next to the bank.
⑰　本屋は 花屋と スーパーの 間に あります。
　　The bookshop is between the florist and the supermarket.

[Note] In the same way as with nouns representing place, the location of an action
can be indicated by attaching the particle で to these.

⑱　駅の 近くで 友達に 会いました。　I met a friend near the station.

5. | N₁や N₂ |

As explained in Lesson 4, the particle と is used to connect nouns in coordinate
relation when enumerating a list of nouns. In contrast to this, the particle や is used
when only a few (two or more) representative items are enumerated. など is
sometimes put after the last noun to make it clear that the speaker has not mentioned
all the nouns that could be on the list.

⑲　箱の 中に 手紙や 写真が あります。
　　There are some letters, photographs and other things in the box.
⑳　箱の 中に 手紙や 写真などが あります。
　　There are some letters, photographs and other things in the box.

6. | アジアストアですか |

The following dialogue occurs at the beginning of this Lesson's conversation:

㉑　すみません。アジアストアは どこですか。
　　……アジアストアですか。（中略） あの ビルの 中です。
　　Excuse me, where is Asia Store?
　　……Asia Store?　(sentence omitted) It's in that building.

In actual conversation, people often do not reply immediately to a question they have
been asked, but first confirm the main point of the question in this way.

Lesson 11

I. Vocabulary

います ［こどもが～］	［子どもが～］	have [a child]
います ［にほんに～］	［日本に～］	stay, be [in Japan]
かかります		take, cost (referring to time or money)
やすみます	休みます	take a day off [work]
［かいしゃを～］	［会社を～］	
ひとつ	1つ	one (used when counting things)
ふたつ	2つ	two
みっつ	3つ	three
よっつ	4つ	four
いつつ	5つ	five
むっつ	6つ	six
ななつ	7つ	seven
やっつ	8つ	eight
ここのつ	9つ	nine
とお	10	ten
いくつ		how many
ひとり	1人	one person
ふたり	2人	two people
－にん	－人	－ people
－だい	－台	(counter for machines, cars, etc.)
－まい	－枚	(counter for paper, stamps, etc.)
－かい	－回	－ times
りんご		apple
みかん		mandarin orange
サンドイッチ		sandwich
カレー［ライス］		curry [with rice]
アイスクリーム		ice cream
きって	切手	postage stamp
はがき		postcard
ふうとう	封筒	envelope
りょうしん	両親	parents
きょうだい	兄弟	brothers and sisters
あに	兄	(my) elder brother

おにいさん*	お兄さん	(someone else's) elder brother
あね	姉	(my) elder sister
おねえさん*	お姉さん	(someone else's) elder sister
おとうと	弟	(my) younger brother
おとうとさん*	弟さん	(someone else's) younger brother
いもうと	妹	(my) younger sister
いもうとさん*	妹さん	(someone else's) younger sister
がいこく	外国	foreign country
りゅうがくせい	留学生	foreign student
クラス		class
―じかん	―時間	― hour(s)
―しゅうかん	―週間	― week(s)
―かげつ	―か月	― month(s)
―ねん	―年	― year(s)
～ぐらい		about ～
どのくらい		how long
ぜんぶで	全部で	in total
みんな		all, everything, everyone
～だけ		only ～

11

〈練習 C〉

かしこまりました。	Certainly, (Sir/Madam).

〈会話〉

いい ［お］天気ですね。	Nice weather, isn't it?
お出かけですか。	Are you going out?
ちょっと ～まで。	I'm just going to ～.
行ってらっしゃい。	See you later./So long. (lit. Go and come back.)
行って きます。	See you later./So long. (lit. I'm going and coming back.)
船便	sea mail
航空便 （エアメール）	airmail
お願いします。	Please. (lit. ask for a favour)

....

オーストラリア	Australia

II. Translation

Sentence Patterns
1. There are seven tables in the meeting room.
2. I'll be (I've been) in Japan for one year.

Example Sentences
1. How many apples did you buy?
   …… [I bought] four.

2. Five eighty-yen stamps and two postcards, please.
   …… Certainly. That'll be five hundred yen altogether.

3. Are there any foreign lecturers at Fuji University?
   …… Yes, there are three. They're all American.

4. How many brothers and sisters do you have?
   …… Three. (lit:Four including me.) Two elder sisters and one elder brother.

5. How many times a week do you play tennis?
   …… [I play] about twice.

6. How long have you been studying Spanish, Mr. Tanaka?
   …… [I've been studying it for] three months.
   Only three months? You're very good at it, aren't you?

7. How long does it take from Osaka to Tokyo on the bullet train?
   …… [It takes] two and a half hours.

11

Conversation

[I'd like to send] this, please

Janitor:	Lovely weather, isn't it? Are you going out?
Wang:	Yes, just to the post office.
Janitor:	Are you? See you later.
Wang:	See you.

………………………………………………………

Wang:	I'd like to send this to Australia, please.
Post Office Clerk:	Of course. Sea mail, or airmail?
Wang:	How much is airmail?
Post Office Clerk:	[It's] ¥7,600.
Wang:	And sea mail?
Post Office Clerk:	[It's] ¥3,450.
Wang:	How long does it take?
Post Office clerk:	Around seven days by air and two months by sea.
Wang:	All right, I'll send it by sea mail, please.

III. Useful Words and Information

メニュー　　**Menu**

ていしょく
定食　　　　　set meal
ランチ　　　　western-style set meal

てん
天どん　　　　a bowl of rice with fried
　　　　　　　seafood and vegetables
おやこ
親子どん　　　a bowl of rice with chicken
　　　　　　　and egg
ぎゅう
牛どん　　　　a bowl of rice with beef

や　にく
焼き肉　　　　grilled meat
やさい
野菜いため　　sautéed vegetables

つけもの
漬物　　　　　pickles
しる
みそ汁　　　　miso soup
おにぎり　　　rice ball

てんぷら　　　fried seafood and vegetables
すし　　　　　vinegared rice with raw fish

うどん　　　　Japanese noodles made from
　　　　　　　wheat flour
そば　　　　　Japanese noodles made from
　　　　　　　buckwheat flour
ラーメン　　　Chinese noodles in soup with
　　　　　　　meat and vegetables

や
焼きそば　　　Chinese stir-fried noodles
　　　　　　　with pork and vegetables
この　や
お好み焼き　　a type of pancake grilled with
　　　　　　　meat, vegetables and egg

カレーライス　curry with rice
ハンバーグ　　hamburg steak
コロッケ　　　croquette
えびフライ　　fried shrimp
フライドチキン　fried chicken

サラダ　　　　salad
スープ　　　　soup
スパゲッティ　spaghetti
ピザ　　　　　pizza
ハンバーガー　hamburger
サンドイッチ　sandwich
トースト　　　toast

コーヒー　　　coffee
こうちゃ
紅茶　　　　　black tea
ココア　　　　cocoa
ジュース　　　juice
コーラ　　　　cola

73

11

IV. Grammar Notes

1. How to say numbers

1) The words ひとつ, ふたつ, ……とお are used to count things up to 10. The numbers themselves are used when counting things from 11 and higher.

2) Counter suffixes

When counting people and things, various different counter suffixes are used depending on what is being counted.

－人 (にん)　　People, except for one and two. One person is counted ひとり (1人), and two people are counted ふたり (2人). 4人 is pronounced よにん.

－台 (だい)　　machines and vehicles

－枚 (まい)　　thin, flat things such as paper, shirts, dishes, and CDs

－回 (かい)　　frequency, number of times

－分 (ふん)　　minutes

－時間 (じかん)　　hours

－日 (にち)　　days

(This is the same as for dates, but 1 日 is pronounced いちにち, not ついたち.)

－週間 (しゅうかん)　　weeks

－か月 (げつ)　　months

－年 (ねん)　　years

2. How to use quantifiers

1) Quantifiers (numbers with counter suffixes) are usually put straight after the noun + particle that determines the type of quantifier. However, this is not always the case with length of time.

① りんごを 4つ 買いました。　　I bought four apples.

② 外国人の 学生が 2人 います。　There are two foreign students.

③ 国で 2か月 日本語を 勉強しました。

　　I studied Japanese for two months in my home country.

2) Asking how many

(1) いくつ

The word いくつ is used when asking how many there are of the items counted by the method explained in 1-1).

④ みかんを いくつ 買いましたか。　How many mandarin oranges did you buy?

　　……8つ 買いました。　　　　　……[I bought] eight.

(2) なん + counter suffix

なん + counter suffix is used when asking how many there are of things with a counter suffix attached as in 1-2).

⑤ この 会社に 外国人が 何人 いますか。
……5人 います。

How many foreign people are there in this company?
…… [There are] five.

⑥ 毎晩 何時間 日本語を 勉強しますか。
……2時間 勉強します。

How many hours do you study Japanese every night?
……[I study for] two hours.

(3) どのくらい

どのくらい is used to ask the length of time something takes.

⑦ どのくらい 日本語を 勉強しましたか。
……3年 勉強しました。

How long did you study Japanese for?
……[I studied it for] three years.

⑧ 大阪から 東京まで どのくらい かかりますか。
……新幹線で 2時間半 かかります。

How long does it take from Osaka to Tokyo?
……[It takes] two and a half hours by Shinkansen.

3) ～ぐらい

ぐらい is added after quantifiers to mean 'about'.

⑨ 学校に 先生が 30人ぐらい います。

There are about thirty teachers at our school.

⑩ 15分ぐらい かかります。　　　　It takes about fifteen minutes.

3. | **Quantifier (time period) に 一回 V** |

This expression indicates frequency.

⑪ 1か月に 2回 映画を 見ます。　　I go to see a film about twice a month.

4. | **Quantifier だけ／ N だけ** |

だけ means 'only'. It is added after quantifiers or nouns to indicate that there is no more or nothing else.

⑫ パワー電気に 外国人の 社員が 1人だけ います。

There is only one foreign employee at Power Electric.

⑬ 休みは 日曜日だけです。　　　　Sunday is my only day off.

Lesson 12

I. Vocabulary

かんたん[な]	簡単[な]	easy, simple
ちかい	近い	near
とおい *	遠い	far
はやい	速い、早い	fast, early
おそい *	遅い	slow, late
おおい [ひとが～]	多い [人が～]	many [people], much
すくない * [ひとが～]	少ない [人が～]	few [people], a little
あたたかい	暖かい、温かい	warm
すずしい	涼しい	cool
あまい	甘い	sweet
からい	辛い	hot (taste), spicy
おもい	重い	heavy
かるい *	軽い	light
いい [コーヒーが～]		prefer [coffee]
きせつ	季節	season
はる	春	spring
なつ	夏	summer
あき	秋	autumn, fall
ふゆ	冬	winter
てんき	天気	weather
あめ	雨	rain, rainy
ゆき	雪	snow, snowy
くもり	曇り	cloudy
ホテル		hotel
くうこう	空港	airport
うみ	海	sea, ocean
せかい	世界	world
パーティー		party（～を します：give a party）
[お]まつり	[お]祭り	festival

すきやき*	すき焼き	sukiyaki (beef and vegetable hot pot)
さしみ*	刺身	sashimi (sliced raw fish)
［お］すし		sushi (vinegared rice topped with raw fish)
てんぷら		tempura (seafood and vegetables deep fried in batter)
ぶたにく*	豚肉	pork
とりにく	とり肉	chicken
ぎゅうにく	牛肉	beef
レモン		lemon
いけばな	生け花	flower arrangement（〜を します： practise flower arrangement）
もみじ	紅葉	maple, red leaves of autumn
どちら		which one (of two things)
どちらも		both
いちばん		the most
ずっと		by far
はじめて	初めて	for the first time

〈会話〉

ただいま。	I'm home.
お帰りなさい。	Welcome home.
わあ、すごい 人ですね。	Wow! Look at all those people!
疲れました。	I'm tired

12

....

祇園 祭	the Gion Festival (the most famous festival in Kyoto)
ホンコン	Hong Kong（香港）
シンガポール	Singapore
ABC ストア	a fictitious supermarket
ジャパン	a fictitious supermarket

II. Translation

Sentence Patterns

1. It was rainy yesterday.
2. It was cold yesterday.
3. Hokkaido is bigger than Kyushu.
4. Summer is my favourite season.

Example Sentences

1. Was Kyoto quiet?
   ……No, it wasn't [quiet].

2. Did you enjoy your trip?
   ……Yes, I did [enjoy it].

   Did you have nice weather?
   ……No, it wasn't very good.

3. How was last night's party?
   ……It was very lively. I met a lot of different people.

4. Is New York colder than Osaka?
   ……Yes, it's much colder.

5. Which takes less time to the airport; the train, or the bus?
   ……The train's quicker.

6. Which do you prefer, the sea or the mountains?
   ……I like them both.

7. Which Japanese dish do you like best?
   ……I like tempura best.

Conversation

How was the Gion Festival?

Miller: I'm back!

Janitor: Welcome back.

Miller: Here's a souvenir from Kyoto.

Janitor: Thank you very much.
      How was the Gion Festival?

Miller: It was interesting.
      It was very lively.

Janitor: That's because the Gion Festival is the most famous of Kyoto's festivals.

Miller: Oh, is it?
      I took a lot of photographs. Take a look.

Janitor: Wow! Look at all those people!

Miller: Yes, it was a bit tiring.

78

12

III. Useful Words and Information

祭りと　名所　　Festivals and Places of Note

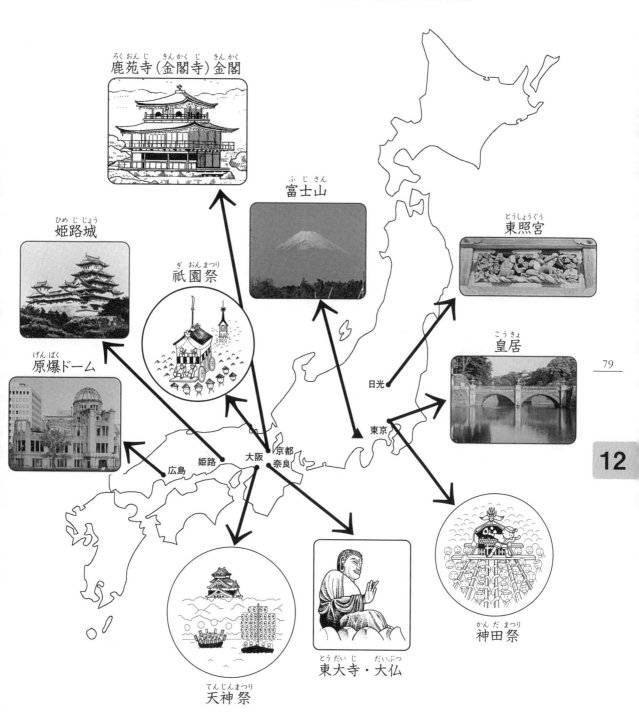

鹿苑寺(金閣寺)金閣

富士山

東照宮

姫路城

祇園祭

皇居

原爆ドーム

日光

東京

京都
奈良

大阪

姫路

広島

天神祭

東大寺・大仏

神田祭

12

IV. Grammar Notes

1. Tense and affirmative/negative forms of noun sentences and な -adjective sentences

	Non-past (present/future)		Past	
Affirmative	N な-adj	あめ しずか } です	N な-adj	あめ しずか } でした
Negative	N な-adj	あめ しずか } じゃ ありません （では）	N な-adj	あめ しずか } じゃ ありませんでした （では）

① きのうは 雨でした。　　　It was rainy yesterday.

② きのうの 試験は 簡単じゃ ありませんでした。
　　Yesterday's exam wasn't easy.

2. Tense and affirmative/negative forms of い -adjective sentences

	Non-past (present/future)	Past
Affirmative	あついです	あつかったです
Negative	あつくないです	あつくなかったです

③ きのうは 暑かったです。　　It was hot yesterday.

④ きのうの パーティーは あまり 楽しくなかったです。
　　I didn't enjoy yesterday's party very much.

3. | N₁ は N₂ より **adj** です |

This sentence pattern describes the quality and/or state of N₁ in comparison with N₂.

⑤ この 車は あの 車より 大きいです。　　This car's bigger than that one.

4. | N₁ と N₂ と どちらが **adj** ですか
……N₁／N₂ の ほうが **adj** です |

The interrogative どちら is used when comparing any two items.

⑥ サッカーと 野球と どちらが おもしろいですか。
　　……サッカーの ほうが おもしろいです。
　　Which [do you think] is more interesting, soccer or baseball?
　　……[I think] soccer's more interesting.

⑦ ミラーさんと サントスさんと どちらが テニスが 上手ですか。
　　Who's better at tennis, Mr. Miller or Mr. Santos?

⑧ 北海道と 大阪と どちらが 涼しいですか。
　　Which is cooler, Hokkaido or Osaka?

⑨ 春と 秋と どちらが 好きですか。
　　Which do you prefer, spring or autumn?

12

5.

$$N_1[の 中]で \begin{Bmatrix} 何 \\ どこ \\ だれ \\ いつ \end{Bmatrix} が いちばん \textbf{adj} ですか$$

$$\cdots\cdots N_2 が いちばん \textbf{adj} です$$

で indicates a range. This question pattern is used to ask the listener to choose, from a group or category denoted by N_1, a thing, place, person, time, etc. that exhibits to the highest degree the state or quality described by the adjective. The interrogative used is determined by the kind of category from which the choice is to be made.

⑩　日本料理[の 中]で 何が いちばん おいしいですか。

　　……てんぷらが いちばん おいしいです。

　　Which of all the Japanese dishes is the most delicious?

　　……Tempura is [the most delicious].

⑪　ヨーロッパで どこが いちばん よかったですか。

　　……スイスが いちばん よかったです。

　　What was your favorite place in Europe?

　　……Switzerland was [the best].

⑫　家族で だれが いちばん 背が 高いですか。

　　……弟が いちばん 背が 高いです。

　　Who is the tallest in your family?

　　……My younger brother is [the tallest]. (See Lesson 16.)

⑬　1年で いつが いちばん 寒いですか。　　What's the coldest time of the year?

　　……2月が いちばん 寒いです。　　　　　……February is [the coldest].

[Note] The particle が is attached to the interrogative even in an interrogative sentence asking about the subject of an adjective sentence (see Lesson 10).

6. Adj の | (の **substituting for a noun**)

Lesson 2 explained the use of の in the form N_1 の to substitute for a noun mentioned previously. The の in the phrase あついの presented in the present lesson's example sentences substitutes for a noun in a similar way, in the form adj の.

⑭　カリナさんの かばんは どれですか。　　Which is Karina's bag?

　　……あの 赤くて、大きいのです。　　……That big red one.

Lesson 13

I. Vocabulary

あそびます	遊びます	enjoy oneself, play
およぎます	泳ぎます	swim
むかえます	迎えます	go to meet, welcome
つかれます	疲れます	get tired (when expressing the condition of being tired, つかれました is used)
けっこんします	結婚します	marry, get married
かいものします	買い物します	do shopping
しょくじします	食事します	have a meal, dine
さんぽします 　[こうえんを〜]	散歩します [公園を〜]	take a walk [in a park]
たいへん[な]	大変[な]	hard, tough, severe, awful
ほしい	欲しい	want (something)
ひろい	広い	wide, spacious
せまい	狭い	narrow, small (room, etc.)
プール		swimming pool
かわ	川	river
びじゅつ	美術	fine arts
つり	釣り	fishing (〜を します：fish, angle)
スキー		skiing (〜を します：ski)
しゅうまつ	週末	weekend
[お]しょうがつ	[お]正月	New Year's Day
〜ごろ		about 〜 (time)
なにか	何か	something
どこか		somewhere, some place

13

のどが かわきます

get thirsty (when expressing the condition of being thirsty, のどが かわきました is used)

おなかが すきます

get hungry (when expressing the condition of being hungry, おなかが すきました is used)

そう しましょう。

Let's do that. (used when agreeing with someone's suggestion)

かいわ
〈会話〉

ちゅうもん
ご注文は?

May I take your order?

ていしょく
定食

set meal, table d´hôte

ぎゅう
牛どん

bowl of rice topped with beef

しょうしょう   ま
[少々] お待ち ください。

Please wait [a moment].

～で ございます。

(polite equivalent of です)

べつべつ
別々に

separately

アキックス

a fictitious company

おはようテレビ

a fictitious TV programme

83

13

II. Translation

Sentence Patterns

1. I want a car.
2. I want to eat some sushi.
3. I'm going to France to study cooking.

Example Sentences

1. What do you want most right now?
   ……[I want] a new mobile phone.

2. Where do you want to go for your summer holiday?
   ……[I want to go to] Okinawa.

3. I feel tired today, so I don't want to do anything.
   ……I understand. Today's meeting was tough, wasn't it?

4. What are you doing at the weekend?
   ……I'm taking the children to Kobe to see the ships.

5. What did you come to study in Japan?
   ……I came to study art.

6. Did you go anywhere for your winter holiday?
   ……Yes, I went skiing in Hokkaido.

Conversation

Separately, please

Yamada: It's twelve o'clock already. Shall we go and have some lunch?
Miller: OK.
Yamada: Where shall we go?
Miller: Hmm...... I'd like to eat something Japanese today.
Yamada: OK, let's go to Tsuruya then.
....

Waitress: What would you like to order?
Miller: The tempura special for me.
Yamada: And I'll have the beef on rice.
Waitress: One tempura special and one beef on rice? Coming right up.
....

Cashier: That's 1,680 yen.
Miller: Sorry, but could we pay separately, please?
Cashier: Of course, the tempura special is 980 yen and the beef on rice is 700 yen.

III. Useful Words and Information

<ruby>町<rt>まち</rt></ruby>の<ruby>中<rt>なか</rt></ruby>　**Town**

<ruby>博物館<rt>はくぶつかん</rt></ruby>　museum

<ruby>美術館<rt>びじゅつかん</rt></ruby>　art museum, art gallery

<ruby>図書館<rt>としょかん</rt></ruby>　library

<ruby>映画館<rt>えいがかん</rt></ruby>　cinema, movie theater

<ruby>動物園<rt>どうぶつえん</rt></ruby>　zoo

<ruby>植物園<rt>しょくぶつえん</rt></ruby>　botanical garden

<ruby>遊園地<rt>ゆうえんち</rt></ruby>　amusement park

<ruby>お寺<rt>てら</rt></ruby>　Buddhist temple

<ruby>神社<rt>じんじゃ</rt></ruby>　Shinto shrine

<ruby>教会<rt>きょうかい</rt></ruby>　Christian church

モスク　Mosque

<ruby>体育館<rt>たいいくかん</rt></ruby>　gymnasium

プール　swimming pool

<ruby>公園<rt>こうえん</rt></ruby>　park

<ruby>大使館<rt>たいしかん</rt></ruby>　embassy

<ruby>入国管理局<rt>にゅうこくかんりきょく</rt></ruby>　immigration bureau

<ruby>市役所<rt>しやくしょ</rt></ruby>　town hall, city hall

<ruby>警察署<rt>けいさつしょ</rt></ruby>　police

<ruby>交番<rt>こうばん</rt></ruby>　police box

<ruby>消防署<rt>しょうぼうしょ</rt></ruby>　fire station

<ruby>駐車場<rt>ちゅうしゃじょう</rt></ruby>　car park, parking lot

<ruby>大学<rt>だいがく</rt></ruby>　university

<ruby>高校<rt>こうこう</rt></ruby>　senior high school

<ruby>中学校<rt>ちゅうがっこう</rt></ruby>　junior high school

<ruby>小学校<rt>しょうがっこう</rt></ruby>　elementary school

<ruby>幼稚園<rt>ようちえん</rt></ruby>　kindergarten

<ruby>肉屋<rt>にくや</rt></ruby>　butcher's shop

<ruby>パン屋<rt>や</rt></ruby>　bakery

<ruby>魚屋<rt>さかなや</rt></ruby>　fishmonger's, fish store

<ruby>酒屋<rt>さかや</rt></ruby>　off-licence, liquor store

<ruby>八百屋<rt>やおや</rt></ruby>　greengrocer's, fruit and vegetable store

<ruby>喫茶店<rt>きっさてん</rt></ruby>　café, coffee shop

コンビニ　convenience store

スーパー　supermarket

デパート　department store

85

13

IV. Grammar Notes

1. | **N が 欲しいです** |

欲しい is an い -adjective, and its object is marked by が .

① わたしは 友達が 欲しいです。   I want some friends.

② 今 何が いちばん 欲しいですか。   What do you want most right now?
…… 車が 欲しいです。   ……I want a car.

③ 子どもが 欲しいですか。   Do you want to have children?
……いいえ、欲しくないです。   ……No, I don't.

2. | **V ます -form たいです** |

1) V ます -form

The form a verb takes when used with ます （e.g. the かい of かいます） is called its ます -form.

2) V ます -form たいです

The pattern V ます -form たいです is used to express the speaker's desire to do something. The object of ～たい can be marked either with the particle を or with the particle が . ～たい inflects in the same way as い -adjectives.

④ わたしは 沖縄へ 行きたいです。   I want to go to Okinawa.

⑤ わたしは てんぷらを 食べたいです。   I'd like to eat some tempura.
             （が）

⑥ 神戸で 何を 買いたいですか。   What do you want to buy in Kobe?
          （が）
…… 靴を 買いたいです。   ……I want to buy some shoes.
    （が）

⑦ おなかが 痛いですから、何も 食べたくないです。

     My stomach hurts, so I don't want to eat anything. (See Lesson 17.)

[Note 1] ほしいです and たいです can only be used when talking about what the speaker or listener wants. They cannot be used to talk about what a third person wants.

[Note 2] Neither ほしいですか nor V ます -form たいですか should be used when offering someone something or inviting them to do something. For example, コーヒーが ほしいですか or コーヒーが のみたいですか are not proper ways of asking someone if they would like a cup of coffee. In this case, an expression such as コーヒーは いかがですか or コーヒーを のみませんか should be used.

3.

$$\text{N (place)} \; \land \; \left\{ \begin{array}{l} \text{V ます -form} \\ \text{N} \end{array} \right\} \; \text{に 行きます／来ます／帰ります}$$

The purposes of the actions いきます, きます and かえります are marked by に.

⑧ 神戸へ インド料理を 食べに 行きます。

   I'm going to Kobe to have some Indian food.

When the verb before に is N します (e.g. かいものします or べんきょうします) or N を します (e.g. おはなみを します or つりを します), it is used in the form N に いきます／きます／かえります.

⑨ 神戸へ 買い物に 行きます。　　　　　I'm going shopping in Kobe.

⑩ 日本へ 美術の 勉強に 来ました。　I came to Japan to study art.

[Note] When a noun denoting an event such as a festival or concert comes before に, the purpose of the action is usually interpreted as being seeing the festival, listening to the concert, etc.

⑪ あした 京都の お祭りに 行きます。

   I'm going to see a festival in Kyoto tomorrow.

4. どこか／何か

どこか means 'anywhere' or 'somewhere', and なにか means 'anything' or 'something'. The particle へ comes after どこか and the particle を after なにか, but either of these can be omitted.

⑫ 冬休みは どこか[へ] 行きましたか。

   ……はい。北海道へ スキーに 行きました。

   Did you go anywhere for your winter holiday?

   ……Yes, I went skiing in Hokkaido.

[Note] は can be added to a word expressing time in order to make it the topic of a sentence.

⑬ のどが かわきましたから、何か[を] 飲みたいです。

   I'm thirsty; I'd like something to drink.

5. ご〜

ご shows respect.

⑭ ご注文は？　　　　　　　　　May I take your order?

87

13

Lesson 14

I. Vocabulary

つけます II		turn on
けします I	消します	turn off
あけます II	開けます	open
しめます II	閉めます	close, shut
いそぎます I	急ぎます	hurry
まちます I	待ちます	wait
もちます I	持ちます	hold
とります I	取ります	take, pass
てつだいます I	手伝います	help (with a task)
よびます I	呼びます	call
はなします I	話します	speak, talk
つかいます I	使います	use
とめます II	止めます	stop, park
みせます II	見せます	show
おしえます II [じゅうしょを～]	教えます [住所を～]	tell [an address]

すわります I	座ります	sit down
たちます I *	立ちます	stand up
はいります I [きっさてんに～]	入ります [喫茶店に～]	enter [a café]
でます II * [きっさてんを～]	出ます [喫茶店を～]	go out [of a café]
ふります I [あめが～]	降ります [雨が～]	rain
コピーします III		copy
でんき	電気	electricity, light
エアコン		air conditioner
パスポート		passport
なまえ	名前	name
じゅうしょ	住所	address
ちず	地図	map
しお	塩	salt
さとう	砂糖	sugar

14

もんだい	問題	question, problem, trouble
こたえ	答え	answer
よみかた	読み方	how to read, way of reading
〜かた	〜方	how to 〜, way of 〜ing
まっすぐ		straight
ゆっくり		slowly, leisurely
すぐ		immediately
また		again
あとで		later
もう すこし	もう 少し	a little more
もう 〜		〜 more, another 〜

〈練習 C〉

| さあ | | right（used when encouraging some course of action） |
| あれ？ | | Oh! Eh?（in surprise or wonder） |

〈会話〉

信号を 右へ 曲がって ください。	Turn right at the traffic lights.
これで お願いします。	I'd like to pay with this.
お釣り	change

· ·

| みどり町 | a fictitious town |

14

II. Translation

Sentence Patterns
1. Just a moment, please.
2. Shall I carry your bag?
3. Mr. Miller's making a phone call now.

Example Sentences
1. Please write your name with a ballpoint pen.
   ······Yes, OK.

2. Excuse me, could you tell me how to read this kanji, please?
   ······It's 'jusho'.

3. Hot, isn't it? Shall I open the window?
   ······Yes, please.

4. Shall I come to the station to meet you?
   ······No, it's fine. I'll get a taxi.

5. Where's Ms. Sato?
   ······She's in the meeting room, talking to Mr. Matsumoto.
   OK, I'll come back later.

6. Is it raining?
   ······No, it isn't [raining].

Conversation
To Midoricho, please

Karina: To Midoricho, please.
Driver: OK.
....

Karina: Excuse me. Please turn right at those lights.
Driver: Right, yes?
Karina: Yes.
....

Driver: Is it straight on?
Karina: Yes, go straight on, please.
....

Karina: Please stop in front of that flower shop.
Driver: OK.
        It's 1,800 yen.
Karina: Take it out of this, please.
Driver: Here's 3,200 yen change. Thank you.

14

III. Useful Words and Information

駅　Station
えき

<table>
<tr><td>切符売り場
きっぷうりば</td><td>ticket office, ticket area</td><td>特急
とっきゅう</td><td>super-express train</td></tr>
<tr><td>自動券売機
じどうけんばいき</td><td>ticket machine</td><td>急行
きゅうこう</td><td>express train</td></tr>
<tr><td>精算機
せいさんき</td><td>fare adjustment machine</td><td>快速
かいそく</td><td>rapid service train</td></tr>
<tr><td>改札口
かいさつぐち</td><td>ticket barrier</td><td>準急
じゅんきゅう</td><td>semi-express train</td></tr>
<tr><td>出口
でぐち</td><td>exit</td><td>普通
ふつう</td><td>local train</td></tr>
<tr><td>入口
いりぐち</td><td>entrance</td><td></td><td></td></tr>
<tr><td>東口
ひがしぐち</td><td>east exit</td><td>時刻表
じこくひょう</td><td>timetable</td></tr>
<tr><td>西口
にしぐち</td><td>west exit</td><td>〜発
はつ</td><td>departing 〜</td></tr>
<tr><td>南口
みなみぐち</td><td>south exit</td><td>〜着
ちゃく</td><td>arriving at 〜</td></tr>
<tr><td>北口
きたぐち</td><td>north exit</td><td>[東京]行き
とうきょう い</td><td>for [TOKYO]</td></tr>
<tr><td>中央口
ちゅうおうぐち</td><td>central exit</td><td></td><td></td></tr>
<tr><td></td><td></td><td>定期券
ていきけん</td><td>season ticket,
commuter pass</td></tr>
<tr><td>[プラット]ホーム</td><td>platform</td><td>回数券
かいすうけん</td><td>coupon ticket</td></tr>
<tr><td>売店
ばいてん</td><td>kiosk</td><td>片道
かたみち</td><td>one way</td></tr>
<tr><td>コインロッカー</td><td>coin locker</td><td>往復
おうふく</td><td>return/round trip</td></tr>
<tr><td>タクシー乗り場
の ば</td><td>taxi rank</td><td></td><td></td></tr>
<tr><td>バスターミナル</td><td>bus terminal</td><td></td><td></td></tr>
<tr><td>バス停
てい</td><td>bus stop</td><td></td><td></td></tr>
</table>

IV. Grammar Notes

1. Verb Groups

Japanese verbs conjugate, and sentences with various meanings can be formed by adding various phrases to the conjugated forms of the verbs. Verbs are classified into three groups depending on how they are conjugated.

1) Group I Verbs

In all verbs of this group, the last sound of the ます -form is from the い -column of the syllabary chart, e.g. か<u>き</u>ます(write), の<u>み</u>ます(drink).

2) Group II verbs

In most verbs of this group, the last sound of the ます -form is from the え -column (e.g. た<u>べ</u>ます (eat) and み<u>せ</u>ます (show)), but in some verbs it is a sound from the い -column (e.g. <u>み</u>ます (see)).

3) Group III Verbs

Verbs of this group include します and 'action-denoting noun ＋します', as well as きます.

2. V て -form

The verb form that ends with て or で is called the て -form. The method by which the て-form is created from the ます -form depends on the group to which the verb belongs, as described below. (See Exercise A1, Lesson14 of Main Text.)

1) Group I Verbs

（1） When the last sound of the ます -form is い, ち or り, the い, ち or り is dropped and って is attached.　　e.g. か<u>い</u>ます　→　かって　buy
ま<u>ち</u>ます　→　まって　wait　　かえ<u>り</u>ます　→　かえって　go home, return

（2） When the last sound of the ます -form is み, び or に, the み, び or に is dropped and んで is attached.　　e.g. の<u>み</u>ます　→　のんで　drink
よ<u>び</u>ます　→　よんで　call　　し<u>に</u>ます　→　しんで　die

（3） When the last sound of the ます -form is き or ぎ, the き or ぎ is dropped and いて or いで respectively is attached.
e.g. か<u>き</u>ます　→　かいて　write　　いそ<u>ぎ</u>ます　→　いそいで　hurry
However いきます (go) is an exception, and becomes いって.

（4） When the last sound of the ます -form is し, て is added to the ます -form.
e.g. か<u>し</u>ます　→　かして　lend

2) Group II Verbs

て is added to the ます -form.　　e.g. た<u>べ</u>ます　→　たべて　eat
み<u>せ</u>ます　→　みせて　show　　<u>み</u>ます　→　みて　see

3) Group III Verbs

て is added to the ます -form.　　e.g. きます　→　きて　come
します　→　して　do　　さんぽします　→　さんぽして　go for a walk

3. ┌ V て -form ください ┐　Please do......

This sentence pattern is used to tell, request or invite the listener to do something.

However, it is not a very polite way of asking someone to do something, so it is often used together with the expression すみませんが as in ① below.

① すみませんが、この 漢字の 読み方を 教えて ください。
　　Excuse me, could you tell me how to read this kanji, please? (Requesting)

② ボールペンで 名前を 書いて ください。
　　Please write your name with a ballpoint pen. (Telling)

③ どうぞ たくさん 食べて ください。　Please eat as much as you want. (Inviting)

4. | **V て -form います** |

This sentence pattern indicates that a certain action or motion is in progress.

④ ミラーさんは 今 電話を かけて います。
　　Mr. Miller is making a phone call now.

⑤ 今 雨が 降って いますか。　　　Is it raining now?
　　……はい、降って います。　　……Yes, it is [raining].
　　……いいえ、降って いません。　……No, it isn't [raining].

5. | **V ます -form ましょうか** |　Shall I......?

This expression is used when the speaker is offering to do something for the listener.

⑥ あしたも 来ましょうか。　　　　Shall I come tomorrow, too?
　　……ええ、10時に 来て ください。　……Yes, please come at ten.

⑦ 傘を 貸しましょうか。　　　　　Shall I lend you my umbrella?
　　……すみません。お願いします。　……Yes, please.

⑧ 荷物を 持ちましょうか。　　　　Shall I carry your bag?
　　……いいえ、けっこうです。　　　……No, thank you.

6. | **N が V** |

When describing a phenomenon by saying what was felt about it through one or more of the five senses (sight, hearing, etc.) or when telling someone objectively about an event, the subject is marked with the particle が.

⑨ 雨が 降って います。　　　　　It's raining.

⑩ ミラーさんが いませんね。　　　Mr. Miller isn't here, is he?

7. | **すみませんが** |

⑪ すみませんが、塩を 取って ください。
　　Excuse me, could you pass the salt, please?

⑫ 失礼ですが、お名前は？　　　　Excuse me, but what is your name?

The が in expressions such as すみませんが and しつれいですが (used as introductory remarks when addressing someone) is not being used in an antithetical sense but as a casual preamble to a remark.

Lesson 15

I. Vocabulary

おきますⅠ	置きます	put
つくりますⅠ	作ります、造ります	make, produce
うりますⅠ	売ります	sell
しりますⅠ	知ります	get to know
すみますⅠ	住みます	be going to live
けんきゅうしますⅢ	研究します	do research
しりょう	資料	materials, data
カタログ		catalogue
じこくひょう	時刻表	timetable
ふく	服	clothes
せいひん	製品	products
ソフト		software
でんしじしょ	電子辞書	electronic dictionary
けいざい	経済	economy
しやくしょ	市役所	municipal office, city hall
こうこう	高校	senior high school
はいしゃ	歯医者	dentist, dentist's
どくしん	独身	single, unmarried
すみません		I'm sorry.

〈練習 C〉
皆さん

Ladies and Gentlemen, everybody

〈会話〉
思い出します I

remember, recollect

いらっしゃいます I

be (honorific equivalent of います)

日本橋

a shopping district in Osaka

みんなの インタビュー

a fictitious TV programme

95

15

II. Translation

Sentence Patterns
1. Is it all right to take photographs?
2. Mr. Santos has an electronic dictionary.

Example Sentences
1. May I have this catalogue, please?
   ······Yes, of course. Please help yourself.

2. May I borrow this dictionary?
   ······Sorry, I'm using it at the moment.

3. You mustn't play here.
   ······Okay.

4. Do you know the ward office's telephone number?
   ······No, I don't.

5. Where does Maria live?
   ······She lives in Osaka.

6. Is Mr. Wang married?
   ······No, he's single.

7. What job do you do?
   ······I'm a teacher. I teach in a secondary school.

Conversation
What family do you have?

Kimura: Good film, wasn't it?

Miller: Yes. It made me think of my family.

Kimura: Oh? What family do you have?

Miller: My parents and one elder sister.

Kimura: Where are they?

Miller: My parents live near New York.
My sister works in London.
How about your family, Ms. Kimura?

Kimura: There are three of us. My father is a bank official.
My mother teaches English in a secondary school.

15

III. Useful Words and Information

<ruby>職業<rt>しょくぎょう</rt></ruby> Occupations

<ruby>会社員<rt>かいしゃいん</rt></ruby> company employee	<ruby>公務員<rt>こうむいん</rt></ruby> civil servant, public servant	<ruby>駅員<rt>えきいん</rt></ruby> station attendant	<ruby>銀行員<rt>ぎんこういん</rt></ruby> bank employee	<ruby>郵便局員<rt>ゆうびんきょくいん</rt></ruby> postman
<ruby>店員<rt>てんいん</rt></ruby> shop assistant	<ruby>調理師<rt>ちょうりし</rt></ruby> cook	<ruby>理容師<rt>りようし</rt></ruby> barber <ruby>美容師<rt>びようし</rt></ruby> beautician	<ruby>教師<rt>きょうし</rt></ruby> teacher	<ruby>弁護士<rt>べんごし</rt></ruby> solicitor, lawyer
<ruby>研究者<rt>けんきゅうしゃ</rt></ruby> research worker	<ruby>医者<rt>いしゃ</rt></ruby>／<ruby>看護師<rt>かんごし</rt></ruby> doctor/nurse	<ruby>運転手<rt>うんてんしゅ</rt></ruby> driver	<ruby>警察官<rt>けいさつかん</rt></ruby> policeman	<ruby>外交官<rt>がいこうかん</rt></ruby> diplomat
<ruby>政治家<rt>せいじか</rt></ruby> politician	<ruby>画家<rt>がか</rt></ruby> painter	<ruby>作家<rt>さっか</rt></ruby> author	<ruby>音楽家<rt>おんがくか</rt></ruby> musician	<ruby>建築家<rt>けんちくか</rt></ruby> architect
エンジニア engineer	デザイナー designer	ジャーナリスト journalist	<ruby>歌手<rt>かしゅ</rt></ruby>／<ruby>俳優<rt>はいゆう</rt></ruby> singer/actor	スポーツ<ruby>選手<rt>せんしゅ</rt></ruby> athlete

15

IV. Grammar Notes

1. | **V て -form も いいですか** |　May I do......?

This sentence pattern is used for asking permission to do something.

① 写真を 撮っても いいですか。　　　　May I take a photo?

② and ③ illustrate how to respond when your permission is sought using this pattern. When withholding permission or stating that something is prohibited, an apologetic or euphemistic answer may be given, or the reason may be given, as illustrated in ② (with holding permission,) and ③ and 2 (stating that something is prohibited) below.

② ここで たばこを 吸っても いいですか。May I smoke here?
　　……ええ、[吸っても] いいですよ。　　　……Yes, you may [smoke].
　　……すみません、ちょっと……。 のどが 痛いですから。
　　……Sorry, I'd prefer it if you didn't. I've got a sore throat. (See Lessson 17.)

③ ここで たばこを 吸っても いいですか。 Is it all right to smoke here?
　　……ええ、[吸っても] いいですよ。　　……Yes, it's fine [to smoke].
　　……いいえ、[吸っては] いけません。 禁煙ですから。
　　……No, it isn't. It's a No Smoking area.

2. | **V て -form は いけません** |　You must not do......

This sentence pattern is used to express prohibition.

④ ここで たばこを 吸っては いけません。禁煙ですから。

　　You can't smoke here; it's a No Smoking area.

This expression cannot be used by someone of lower status to someone of higher status.

3. | **V て -form います** |

This sentence pattern is used in the ways illustrated below, in addition to expressing a continuing action as explained in Lesson 14.

1) To show a state （mainly with verbs used in the ～て います form）

⑤ わたしは 結婚して います。　　　　I'm married.
⑥ わたしは 田中さんを 知って います。 I know Mr. Tanaka.
⑦ わたしは カメラを 持って います。　 I have a camera.
⑧ わたしは 大阪に 住んで います。　　 I live in Osaka.

[Note 1] The negative of しって います is しりません. Be careful not to say しって いません.

⑨ 市役所の 電話番号を 知って いますか。

　　Do you know the number of City Hall?

　　……はい、知って います。　　　　……Yes, I do.
　　……いいえ、知りません。　　　　……No, I don't.

[Note 2] The phrase もって います can mean either having something with you at the moment, or owning it.

2) To show a habitual action (the same action repeated over a long period), occupation or personal status.

⑩ IMC は コンピューターソフトを 作って います。
IMC produces computer software.

⑪ スーパーで ナンプラーを 売って います。　Supermarkets sell nam pla.

⑫ ミラーさんは IMC で 働いて います。　　Mr. Miller works at IMC.

⑬ 妹 は 大学で 勉強して います。
My younger sister is studying at university.

4. | Nに V |

The particle に is used with verbs such as はいります, すわります, のります (ride; see Lesson 16), のぼります (climb, go up; see Lesson 19) and つきます (arrive; see Lesson 25) to indicate the location of the subject resulting from the action expressed by the verb.

⑭ ここに 入っては いけません。　　　　You can't come in here.

⑮ ここに 座っても いいですか。　　　　May I sit here?

⑯ 京都駅から 16番の バスに 乗って ください。
Take the Number 16 bus from Kyoto Station. (See Lesson 16.)

5. | N₁に N₂を V |

The particle に indicates the location (N₁) of N₂ as the result of an action.

⑰ ここに 車を 止めて ください。　　　　Stop the car here, please.

The に in ⑱ has the same function.

⑱ ここに 住所を 書いて ください。　　　Write your address here, please.

15

Lesson 16

I. Vocabulary

のりますⅠ 　［でんしゃに～］	乗ります 　［電車に～］	ride, get on [a train]
おりますⅡ 　［でんしゃを～］	降ります 　［電車を～］	get off [a train]
のりかえますⅡ	乗り換えます	change（train, etc.）
あびますⅡ 　［シャワーを～］	浴びます	take [a shower]
いれますⅡ	入れます	put in, insert
だしますⅠ	出します	take out, hand in, send
おろしますⅠ 　［おかねを～］	下ろします 　［お金を～］	withdraw
はいりますⅠ 　［だいがくに～］	入ります 　［大学に～］	enter [university]
でますⅡ 　［だいがくを～］	出ます 　［大学を～］	graduate from [university]
おしますⅠ	押します	push, press
のみますⅠ	飲みます	drink alcohol
はじめますⅡ	始めます	start, begin
けんがくしますⅢ	見学します	tour, visit a place to study it
でんわしますⅢ	電話します	phone
わかい	若い	young
ながい	長い	long
みじかい	短い	short
あかるい	明るい	bright, light
くらい	暗い	dark
からだ*	体	body, health
あたま	頭	head, brain
かみ	髪	hair
かお*	顔	face
め	目	eye
みみ*	耳	ear
はな*	鼻	nose
くち*	口	mouth
は*	歯	tooth
おなか*		stomach
あし*	足	leg, foot
せ	背	height

サービス		service
ジョギング		jogging（〜を します：jog）
シャワー		shower
みどり	緑	green, greenery
［お］てら	［お］寺	Buddhist temple
じんじゃ	神社	Shinto shrine
－ばん	－番	number －
どうやって		in what way, how
どの 〜		which 〜（used for three or more）
どれ		which one（of three or more things）

〈練習 C〉

すごいですね。　That's amazing!

［いいえ、］まだまだです。　[No,] I still have a long way to go.

〈会話〉

お引き出しですか。	Are you making a withdrawal?
まず	first of all
次に	next, as a next step
キャッシュカード	cash dispensing card
暗証番号	personal identification number, PIN
金額	amount of money
確認	confirmation（〜します：confirm）
ボタン	button

101

- -

JR	Japan Railways
雪祭り	Snow Festival
バンドン	Bandung（in Indonesia）
フランケン	Franken（in Germany）
ベラクルス	Veracruz（in Mexico）
梅田	a district in Osaka
大学前	a fictitious bus stop

16

II. Translation

Sentence Patterns

1. In the mornings, I go jogging, have a shower, and then go to work.
2. After the concert was over, we had a meal in a restaurant.
3. The food in Osaka is very good.
4. This room is big and bright.

Example Sentences

1. What did you do yesterday?
   ······I went to the library, borrowed a book, and then met some friends.

2. How do you get to the University?
   ······I get on the number 16 bus at Kyoto station and get off at Daigakumae.

3. Are you going to look round Osaka Castle now?
   ······No, we're going there after lunch.

4. Which is Maria?
   ······She's the one with long hair over there.

5. Which is Taro's bike?
   ······It's that new blue one.

6. What sort of city is Nara?
   ······It's a quiet, beautiful city.

7. Who's that person over there?
   ······That's Karina. She's Indonesian, and she's a student at Fuji University.

Conversation

Please show me how to use it

Maria:	Excuse me, could you show me how to use this, please?
Bank official:	Do you want to take some money out?
Maria:	Yes.
Bank official:	Right, start by pressing here, please.
Maria:	OK.
Bank official:	Then put your cash card in here and type in your pin number.
Maria:	OK.
	I've done that.
Bank official:	OK, now press the amount you want.
Maria:	I want 50,000 yen, so 5······
Bank official:	Press this 'Man (10,000)' key and the 'En (YEN)' key here.
	Then press this 'Kakunin (CONFIRM)' button.
Maria:	Yes. Thank you very much.

III. Useful Words and Information

ATM の 使い方　How to Use a Cash Machine

お預け入れ　deposit
お振り込み　payment
お振り替え　transfer
お引き出し　withdrawal
通帳記入　updating your passbook
残高照会　balance inquiry

暗証番号
personal identification number (PIN)

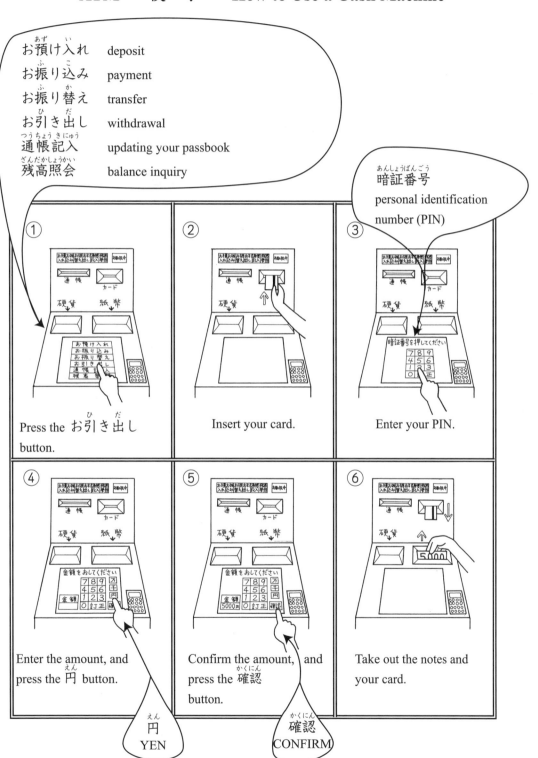

① Press the お引き出し button.

② Insert your card.

③ Enter your PIN.

④ Enter the amount, and press the 円 button.

⑤ Confirm the amount, and press the 確認 button.

⑥ Take out the notes and your card.

円
YEN

確認
CONFIRM

103

16

IV. Grammar Notes

1. How to join two or more sentences together

Two or more sentences can be joined together using ～て（で）.

1) V₁ て -form、［V₂ て -form、］V₃

When mentioning two or more actions that take place in succession, they are listed in their order of occurrence using the て -form. The tense of the sentence is determined by the tense form of the last verb in the sentence.

① 朝 ジョギングを して、シャワーを 浴びて、会社へ 行きます。

In the mornings, I go jogging, take a shower, and then go to work.

② 神戸へ 行って、映画を 見て、お茶を 飲みました。

I went to Kobe, where I saw a movie and drank some tea.

2) い -adj（～い̸）　→　～くて

おおきーい　→　おおきーくて　　　　　　big

ちいさーい　→　ちいさーくて　　　　　　small

いーい　→　　　よーくて（exception）　good

③ ミラーさんは 若くて、元気です。　　Mr. Miller is young and energetic.

④ きのうは 天気が よくて、暑かったです。　It was fine and hot yesterday.

3) な -adj［な］　→　～で

⑤ ミラーさんは ハンサムで、親切です。　Mr. Miller is handsome and kind.

⑥ 奈良は 静かで、きれいな 町です。　　Nara is a quiet, beautiful city.

[Note] ～て（で）cannot be used to connect two adjective sentences having the same subject if they present two contrasting descriptions. In such a case, が is used (see Lesson 8-4).

　　×この 部屋は 狭くて、きれいです。

　　○この 部屋は 狭いですが、きれいです。　This room is small but clean.

4) N で

⑦ カリナさんは インドネシア人で、富士大学の 留学生です。

Karina is Indonesian; she's a student at Fuji University.

⑧ カリナさんは 学生で、マリアさんは 主婦です。

Karina is a student, and Maria is a housewife.

2. V₁ て -form から、V₂

In this sentence pattern, V₂ expresses something done after V₁. Because of this, V₁ is often a precondition of doing V₂ or an action preparatory to doing it. The tense of the sentence is determined by the tense of the last verb in the sentence.

⑨ お金を 入れてから、ボタンを 押して ください。

Put the money in, please, and then press the button.

The subject of V て -form から is marked with the particle が.

⑩　もう 昼ごはんを 食べましたか。　Have you already had your lunch?

　　……この 仕事が 終わってから、食べます。

　　……No, I'm going to have it when I've finished this job.

3. | N₁ は N₂ が adj |

This sentence pattern indicates that the topic (N₁) has the characteristic 'N₂ が adj'.

⑪　大阪は 食べ物が おいしいです。　The food in Osaka is very good.

⑫　ドイツの フランケンは ワインが 有名です。

　　Franken in Germany is famous for its wine.

⑬　マリアさんは 髪が 長いです。　　Maria has long hair.

4. | N を V |

Verbs such as でます and おります, are used together with the particle を , which indicates a starting point.

⑭　7時に うちを 出ます。　　　　I leave home at seven.

⑮　梅田で 電車を 降りました。　　I got off the train at Umeda.

5. | どうやって |

どうやって is used when asking the way or how to do something.

⑯　大学まで どうやって 行きますか。

　　How do you get to the University?

　　……京都駅から 16番の バスに 乗って、大学前で 降ります。

　　……I take the Number 16 bus from Kyoto Station and get off at Daigakumae.

6. | どれ／どの N |

どれ is an interrogative used when asking someone to specify one item out of a list of three or more .

⑰　ミラーさんの 傘は どれですか。　Which is Mr. Miller's umbrella?

　　……あの 青い 傘です。　　　　……It's that blue one.

どれ cannot modify a noun directly. When modifying a noun, どの is used.

⑱　サントスさんは どの 人ですか。　Which is Mr. Santos?

　　……あの 背が 高くて、髪が 黒い 人です。

　　……That tall, black-haired man.

16

Lesson 17

I. Vocabulary

おぼえます II	覚えます	memorise
わすれます II	忘れます	forget
なくします I		lose
はらいます I	払います	pay
かえします I	返します	give back, return
でかけます II	出かけます	go out
ぬぎます I	脱ぎます	take off (clothes, shoes, etc.)

もって いきます I	持って 行きます	take (something)
もって きます III	持って 来ます	bring (something)
しんぱいします III	心配します	worry
ざんぎょうします III	残業します	work overtime
しゅっちょうします III	出張します	go on a business trip
のみます I [くすりを〜]	飲みます [薬を〜]	take [medicine]
はいります I [おふろに〜]	入ります	take [a bath]

たいせつ[な]	大切[な]	important, precious
だいじょうぶ[な]	大丈夫[な]	all right

あぶない	危ない	dangerous

きんえん	禁煙	no smoking

[けんこう] ほけんしょう	[健康]保険証	[health] insurance card

ねつ	熱	temperature, fever
びょうき	病気	illness, disease
くすり	薬	medicine

[お]ふろ		bath

うわぎ	上着	jacket, outerwear
したぎ	下着	underwear

2、3にち	2、3日	two or three days
2、3～		two or three ～ (where ～ is a counter suffix)
～までに		before ～, by ～ (indicating time limit)
ですから		therefore, so

〈会話〉

どう しましたか。	What's the matter?
のど	throat
[～が] 痛いです。	(I) have a pain [in my ～].
かぜ	cold, flu
それから	and, furthermore
お大事に。	Take care of yourself. (said to people who are ill)

17

II. Translation

Sentence Patterns
1. Please don't take photographs.
2. You have to show your passport.
3. I don't have to get up early on Sundays.

Example Sentences
1. Please don't park there.
   ······Sorry.

2. It's already midnight. Will you be all right on your own?
   ······Yes, please don't worry; I'll take a taxi home.

3. Shall we go out for a drink tonight?
   ······Sorry, I have to go on a business trip to Hong Kong tomorrow, so I'm going home early.

4. Do children have to pay, too?
   ······No, they don't [have to pay].

5. When does the report have to be handed in by?
   ······[Hand it in] by Friday, please.

Conversation

What seems to be the matter?

Doctor:	What seems to be the matter?
Matsumoto:	I've had a sore throat since yesterday, and I've also got a slight temperature.
Doctor:	I see. Say, "Aah", please. (lit:Open your mouth a moment, please.)

··

Doctor:	You've caught a cold, haven't you? Please take it easy for two or three days.
Matsumoto:	Yes, but I have to go to Tokyo on business tomorrow.
Doctor:	OK, please take your medicine and go to bed early today.
Matsumoto:	All right.
Doctor:	And please don't have a bath tonight, OK?
Matsumoto:	Yes, I understand.
Doctor:	Right you are then, look after yourself.
Matsumoto:	Thank you very much.

17

III. Useful Words and Information

<ruby>体<rt>からだ</rt></ruby>・<ruby>病気<rt>びょうき</rt></ruby> **Body and Illness**

どう しましたか。	What seems to be the problem?
<ruby>頭<rt>あたま</rt></ruby>が <ruby>痛<rt>いた</rt></ruby>い	have a headache
おなかが <ruby>痛<rt>いた</rt></ruby>い	have a stomachache
<ruby>歯<rt>は</rt></ruby>が <ruby>痛<rt>いた</rt></ruby>い	have a toothache
<ruby>熱<rt>ねつ</rt></ruby>が あります	have a temperature, fever
せきが <ruby>出<rt>で</rt></ruby>ます	have a cough
<ruby>鼻水<rt>はなみず</rt></ruby>が <ruby>出<rt>で</rt></ruby>ます	have a runny nose
<ruby>血<rt>ち</rt></ruby>が <ruby>出<rt>で</rt></ruby>ます	bleed
<ruby>吐<rt>は</rt></ruby>き<ruby>気<rt>け</rt></ruby>が します	feel sick, nauseous
<ruby>寒気<rt>さむけ</rt></ruby>が します	feel a chill
めまいが します	feel dizzy
<ruby>下痢<rt>げり</rt></ruby>を します	have diarrhoea
<ruby>便秘<rt>べんぴ</rt></ruby>を します	be constipated
けがを します	get injured
やけどを します	get burnt
<ruby>食欲<rt>しょくよく</rt></ruby>が ありません	have no appetite
<ruby>肩<rt>かた</rt></ruby>が こります	feel stiff in one's shoulders
<ruby>体<rt>からだ</rt></ruby>が だるい	feel weary
かゆい	itchy

かお　あたま　め　はな　かみ　くち　みみ　のど　あご　くび　ゆび　むね　かた　うで　て　ひじ　せなか　つめ　ひざ　おなか　こし　ほね　あし　しり

109

17

かぜ	cold	ぎっくり<ruby>腰<rt>ごし</rt></ruby>	slipped disc
インフルエンザ	flu, influenza	ねんざ	sprain
<ruby>盲腸<rt>もうちょう</rt></ruby>	appendicitis	<ruby>骨折<rt>こっせつ</rt></ruby>	bone fracture
		<ruby>二日酔<rt>ふつかよ</rt></ruby>い	hangover

IV. Grammar Notes

1. V ない -form

The form of a verb that attaches to ない (e.g. かか in かかない) is called its ない-form. The method by which the ない -form is created from the ます -form depends on the group to which the verb belongs, as explained below. （See Exercise A1, Lesson 17 of Main Text.）

1） Group I Verbs

The final sound of the ます-form of verbs in this group is always from the い -column, and this is changed to the corresponding syllable from the あ-column to make the ない -form. However, with verbs where the final sound is the vowel い （e.g. かいます and あいます）, this changes not to あ but to わ.

かき－ます	→	かか－ない	いそぎ－ます	→	いそが－ない
よみ－ます	→	よま－ない	あそび－ます	→	あそば－ない
とり－ます	→	とら－ない	まち－ます	→	また－ない
すい－ます	→	すわ－ない	はなし－ます	→	はなさ－ない

2） Group II Verbs

The ない -form of verbs in this group is the same as their ます -form.

たべ－ます → たべ－ない

み－ます → み－ない

3） Group III Verbs

べんきょうし－ます → べんきょうし－ない

し－ます → し－ない

き－ます → こ－ない

2. | V ない -form ないで ください | Please don't do......

This sentence pattern is used to ask or tell someone not to do something.

① ここで 写真を 撮らないで ください。

Please don't take photographs here.

It can also be used to show consideration to someone by telling them they don't have to do something.

② わたしは 元気ですから、心配しないで ください。

I'm fine, so please don't worry about me.

3. | V ない -form なければ なりません | Must do......

This sentence pattern is used to say that something must be done. Note that it is not in the negative.

③ 薬を 飲まなければ なりません。   I must take some medicine.

110

17

4. | **V ない -form なくても いいです** | Need not do......

This sentence pattern is used when saying that it is not necessary to do something.

④ あした 来_こなくても いいです。 You don't have to come tomorrow.

5. Making an object the topic of a sentence

When making a noun in the expression N を V (i.e. a noun that is the direct object of a verb) into the topic of a sentence, the noun is placed at the beginning of the sentence and the particle を is replaced by the particle は .

ここに 荷物_{にもつ}を 置_おかないで ください。 Don't put your bags here, please.

荷物_{にもつ}をは ここに 置_おかないで ください。

⑤ 荷物_{にもつ}は ここに 置_おかないで ください。 Don't put your bags here, please.

会社_{かいしゃ}の 食堂_{しょくどう}で 昼_{ひる}ごはんを 食_たべます。

I have lunch in the company cafeteria.

昼_{ひる}ごはんをは 会社_{かいしゃ}の 食堂_{しょくどう}で 食_たべます。

⑥ 昼_{ひる}ごはんは 会社_{かいしゃ}の 食堂_{しょくどう}で 食_たべます。

I have lunch in the company cafeteria.

6. | **N(time)までに V** |

This indicates a time by which an event will end or an action must be completed.

⑦ 会議_{かいぎ}は 5時_じまでに 終_おわります。 The meeting will end by five.

⑧ 土曜日_{どようび}までに 本_{ほん}を 返_{かえ}さなければ なりません。

I have to return the book by Saturday.

[Note] The particle まで explained in Lesson 4 indicates the end point of a continuing action. Be careful not to confuse it with までに.

⑨ 5時_じまで 働_{はたら}きます。 I work until five o'clock.

Lesson 18

I. Vocabulary

できますⅡ		be able to, can
あらいますⅠ	洗います	wash
ひきますⅠ	弾きます	play (stringed instrument, piano, etc.)
うたいますⅠ	歌います	sing
あつめますⅡ	集めます	collect, gather
すてますⅡ	捨てます	throw away
かえますⅡ	換えます	exchange, change
うんてんしますⅢ	運転します	drive
よやくしますⅢ	予約します	reserve, book
ピアノ		piano
ーメートル		－ meter
げんきん	現金	cash
しゅみ	趣味	hobby
にっき	日記	diary
おいのり	お祈り	prayer (〜を します：pray)
かちょう	課長	section head
ぶちょう	部長	department head
しゃちょう*	社長	company president
どうぶつ	動物	animal
うま	馬	horse
インターネット		the Internet

特に　especially

へえ　What! Really! (used when expressing surprise)

それは おもしろいですね。　That's interesting, isn't it?

なかなか　not easily (used with negatives)

ほんとうですか。　Really?

ぜひ　by all means, really

故郷　Furusato (a song title meaning 'Home Town')

ビートルズ　the Beatles (a famous British pop group)

秋葉原　a district in Tokyo

113

18

II. Translation

Sentence Patterns

1. Mr. Miller can read kanji.
2. I like watching films. [lit: My hobby is watching films.]
3. I always write something in my diary before I go to sleep.

Example Sentences

1. Can you drive?
   ······Yes, I can.

2. Can you ride a bike, Maria?
   ······No, I can't.

3. What time is Osaka Castle open until?
   ······[Until] five o'clock.

4. Can I pay by card?
   ······I'm sorry, we only take cash.

5. What are you interested in? [lit: What are your hobbies?]
   ······I collect old clocks.

6. Do Japanese children have to learn hiragana before they start school?
   ······No, they don't [have to learn it].

7. Please take this medicine before meals.
   ······Yes, I understand.

8. When did you get married?
   ······[I got married] three years ago.

Conversation

What do you like doing? [lit: What are your hobbies?]

Yamada: What do you like doing, Mr. Santos?

Santos: Photography.

Yamada: What kind of photographs do you take?

Santos: Photographs of animals. I particularly like horses.

Yamada: Really? How interesting!
Have you photographed any horses since coming to Japan?

Santos: No.
You don't see many horses in Japan.

Yamada: There are a lot of horses in Hokkaido, you know.

Santos: Really?
In that case, I definitely want to go there during my summer holiday.

III. Useful Words and Information

動き Actions

飛ぶ fly	跳ぶ jump	登る climb	走る run
泳ぐ swim	もぐる dive	飛び込む dive into	逆立ちする do a handstand
はう crawl	ける kick	振る wave	持ち上げる lift
投げる throw	たたく pat, tap	引く pull	押す push
曲げる bend	伸ばす extend	転ぶ fall down	振り向く look back

115

18

IV. Grammar Notes

1. Dictionary form of verbs

This is the basic form of a verb, as given in the dictionary. The method by which the dictionary form is created from the ます-form depends on which group the verb belongs to, as explained below. (See Exercise A1, Lesson 18, Main Textbook.)

1) Group I verbs

With verbs in this group, the last sound of the ます-form, which is always in the い -column, is changed to a corresponding sound in the う -column.

かき－ます → かく　　いそぎ－ます → いそぐ
よみ－ます → よむ　　あそび－ます → あそぶ
とり－ます → とる　　　まち－ます → 　まつ
すい－ます → すう　　はなし－ます → はなす

2) Group II verbs

る is added to the ます -form.

たべ－ます → たべる
み－ます → 　みる

3) Group III verbs

The dictionary form of します is する , while that of きます is くる .

2.

| N
V-dictionary form こと } が できます | Can do...... |

できます is a verb that indicates that a person has the ability to do something or that some behaviour is possible as a result of the situation. The object of できます is marked by が , and the ability or what is possible is expressed in the form of either a noun or the dictionary form of a verb with こと added to it.

1) In the case of a noun

Nouns indicating motion, such as（うんてん , かいもの , スキー and ダンス）can be used, as can nouns representing an ability, such as にほんご or ピアノ .

① ミラーさんは 日本語が できます。

Mr. Miller can speak Japanese.

② 雪が たくさん 降りましたから、ことしは スキーが できます。

A lot of snow has fallen, so we can ski this year.

2) In the case of a verb

When a verb is used to describe an ability or possibility, こと is attached to the verb's dictionary form to make it a noun phrase, which is then followed by が できます .

③ ミラーさんは 漢字を 読む ことが できます。　Mr. Miller can read kanji.
　　　　　　　　(noun phrase)

④ カードで 払う ことが できます。　　　　　You can pay by card.
　 (noun phrase)

3.

$$わたしの \, 趣味は \begin{Bmatrix} \textbf{N} \\ \textbf{V-dictionary form} \, こと \end{Bmatrix} です$$

My interest is......

⑤ わたしの 趣味は 音楽です。　　　　I'm interested in music.

Using the V-dictionary form こと enables the interest to be described more specifically than just using a noun.

⑥ わたしの 趣味は 音楽を 聞く ことです。　I like listening to music.

4.

$$\begin{Bmatrix} \textbf{V}_1\textbf{-dictionary form} \\ \textbf{N} \, の \\ \textbf{Quantifier (time period)} \end{Bmatrix} まえに、\textbf{V}_2$$

......before......

1) Verb

This sentence pattern shows that V_2 occurs before V_1. Note that V_1 always takes the dictionary form whether the tense of the sentence (i.e. the tense of V_2) is past or non-past.

⑦ 日本へ 来る まえに、日本語を 勉強 しました。

I studied Japanese before coming to Japan.

⑧ 寝る まえに、本を 読みます。　　　I read a book before going to bed.

2) Noun

の is added after the noun. Nouns expressing motion can be used.

⑨ 食事の まえに、手を 洗います。　　I wash my hands before eating.

3) Quantifier (time period)

Note that の is not added to a quantifier (time period).

⑩ 田中さんは 1時間まえに、出かけました。 Mr. Tanaka went out one hour ago.

5. なかなか

When なかなか is followed by a negative expression, it means 'not easily' or 'not as expected'.

⑪ 日本では なかなか 馬を 見る ことが できません。

You don't see many horses in Japan.

[Note] Example sentence ⑪ (see Conversation, Lesson 18 of Main Text) takes にほんで as its topic. When a noun with で attached is taken as the topic in this way, it becomes Nでは. (See Article 1 for what happens when words with particles other than が and を are taken as sentence topics.)

6. ぜひ

ぜひ is used by speakers to intensify their expressions of hope.

⑫ ぜひ 北海道へ 行きたいです。　　　I really want to go to Hokkaido.

⑬ ぜひ 遊びに 来て ください。　　　Do please come and visit me.

Lesson 19

I. Vocabulary

のぼります I	登ります、上ります	climb, go up
とまります I	泊まります	stay [at a hotel]
［ホテルに〜］		
そうじします III	掃除します	clean (a room)
せんたくします III	洗濯します	wash (clothes)
なります I		become
ねむい	眠い	sleepy
つよい	強い	strong
よわい*	弱い	weak
れんしゅう	練習	practice（〜［を］します：practise）
ゴルフ		golf（〜を します：play golf）
すもう	相撲	sumo wrestling（〜を します：wrestle）
おちゃ	お茶	tea ceremony
ひ	日	day, date
ちょうし	調子	condition
いちど	一度	once
いちども	一度も	not once, never (used with negatives)
だんだん		gradually
もうすぐ		soon
おかげさまで		Thank you.（used when expressing gratitude for help received）
でも		but

〈**会話**〉

乾杯　　　　　　　　　　Bottoms up./Cheers!

ダイエット　　　　　　　diet（〜を　します：go on a diet）

無理[な]　　　　　　　　excessive, impossible

体に　いい　　　　　　　good for one's health

....

東京スカイツリー　　　　Tokyo Sky Tree（broadcasting tower
　　　　　　　　　　　　　　with observation deck in Tokyo）

葛飾北斎　　　　　　　　a famous Edo-period woodblock artist
　　　　　　　　　　　　　　and painter（1760-1849）

19

II. Translation

Sentence Patterns

1. I've been to see sumo.
2. On my days off, I do things like playing tennis and going for a walk.
3. It's going to get hotter and hotter from now on.

Example Sentences

1. Have you ever been to Hokkaido?

    ······Yes, once. I went there two years ago with some friends.

2. Have you ever ridden a horse?

    ······No, never, but I'd really like to.

3. What did you do during your winter holiday?

    ······I went to temples, shrines and other places in Kyoto, partied with my friends, and so on.

4. What do you want to do in Japan?

    ······I want to travel around, study the tea ceremony, and other things.

5. How are you feeling?

    ······Better, thank you.

6. You've got very good at Japanese, haven't you?

    ······Thank you, but I've still got a long way to go.

7. What you want to be when you grow up, Teresa?

    ······I want to be a doctor.

Conversation

I'll start dieting tomorrow

Everybody:	Cheers!
	··
Yoshiko Matsumoto:	You're not eating much, are you, Maria?
Maria:	No, I've been on a diet since yesterday.
Yoshiko Matsumoto:	I see. I've been on some diets, too.
Maria:	What sort of diets?
Yoshiko Matsumoto:	Like only eating apples every day, and drinking lots of water. But over-strict diets aren't good for you, are they?
Maria:	No, they aren't.
Yoshiko Matsumoto:	This ice cream very nice, Maria.
Maria:	Is it? ...... OK, I'll start dieting again tomorrow.

19

III. Useful Words and Information

伝統文化・娯楽　Traditional Culture and Entertainment

茶道 tea ceremony（お茶）

華道 flower arranging（生け花）

書道 calligraphy

歌舞伎 Kabuki

能 Noh

文楽 Bunraku

相撲 sumo

柔道 judo

剣道 kendo

空手 karate

漫才・落語 manzai, rakugo

囲碁・将棋 go, shogi

パチンコ pachinko

カラオケ karaoke

盆踊り Bon dance

19

IV. Grammar Notes

1. V た -form

Forms of verbs ending in た or だ are called their た-form. A verb's た -form is created by changing the て or で of its て -form to た or だ respectively. (See Exercise A1, Lesson 19 of Main Text.)

て -form → た -form
かいて → かいた
のんで → のんだ
たべて → たべた
きて → きた
して → した

2. | V た **-form** こと が あります |　have the experience of V-ing

This sentence pattern is used to say that one has had a particular experience, without saying when that experience occurred.

① 馬に 乗った ことが あります。　　I've ridden a horse.

Note that the past tense is used when simply mentioning something that happened in the past.

② 去年 北海道で 馬に 乗りました。　I rode a horse last year in Hokkaido.

3. | V₁ た **-form** り、V₂ た **-form** り します |　V₁, V₂ and so on......

As already explained, the particle や is used when citing two or more nouns as typical examples from a longer list. This sentence pattern is used when doing the same with verbs. The tense is shown at the end of the sentence.

③ 日曜日は テニスを したり、映画を 見たり します。

On Sundays, I play tennis, watch a film, and so on.

④ 日曜日は テニスを したり、映画を 見たり しました。

Last Sunday, I played tennis, watched a film and did some other stuff.

[Note] Be sure not to confuse this sentence pattern with the V₁ て -form、[V₂ て -form、] V₃ sentence pattern presented in Lesson 16, which is used to enumerate all the members of a list of two or more successive actions in their order of occurrence.

⑤ 日曜日は テニスを して、映画を 見ました。

On Sunday, I played tennis and then watched a film.

Unlike with this sentence pattern, V₁ た -form り、V₂ た -form り します is used to enumerate a few typical actions from a longer list, indicating no time relationship between them. Because it is used to list actions non-exhaustively, it would be unnatural to use it for mentioning actions that everyone usually does every day, such as getting up in the morning, eating meals, and going to bed at night.

122

19

4.

$$\left.\begin{array}{l} \text{い -adj}\,(\sim\cancel{\text{い}}) \;\rightarrow\; \sim\text{く} \\ \text{な -adj}\,[\cancel{\text{な}}] \;\rightarrow\; \sim\text{に} \\ \text{N\;に} \end{array}\right\} \text{なります}$$ become......

なります indicates a change of state.

⑥ 寒い → 寒く なります   Get cold.

⑦ 元気[な] → 元気に なります   Get better.

⑧ 25歳 → 25歳に なります   Turn 25 [years old].

19

Lesson 20

I. Vocabulary

いります I 　[ビザが〜]	要ります	need, require [a visa]
しらべます II	調べます	check, investigate
しゅうりします III	修理します	repair
ぼく	僕	I（an informal equivalent of わたし used by men）
きみ*	君	you（an informal equivalent of あなた used to address people of equal or lower status）
〜くん	〜君	Mr.（an informal equivalent of 〜さん used to address people of equal or lower status; also often appended to boys' names）
うん		yes（an informal equivalent of はい）
ううん		no（an informal equivalent of いいえ）
ことば		word, language
きもの	着物	kimono（traditional Japanese attire）
ビザ		visa
はじめ	初め	the beginning
おわり	終わり	the end of 〜, The End
こっち*		this way, this place（an informal equivalent of こちら）
そっち		that way, that place near the listener（an informal equivalent of そちら）
あっち*		that way, that place over there（an informal equivalent of あちら）
どっち		which one（of two things）, which way, where（an informal equivalent of どちら）
みんなで		all together
〜けど		〜, but（an informal equivalent of が）
おなかが いっぱいです		（I'm）full

〈**会話**〉

| よかったら | if you like |
| いろいろ | various |

II. Translation

Sentence Patterns
1. Mr. Santos didn't come to the party.
2. There are a lot of people in Tokyo.
3. The sea in Okinawa was beautiful.
4. It's my birthday today.

Example Sentences
1. Like some ice cream?
   ······Yes, I would.

2. Do you have any scissors there?
   ······No, I don't.

3. Did you meet Ms. Kimura yesterday?
   ······No, I didn't.

4. Is that curry good?
   ······Yes, it's spicy, but it tastes nice.

5. Shall we all go to Kyoto tomorrow?
   ······Yes, that sounds good.

6. What would you like to eat?
   ······I'm full up at the moment, so I don't want to eat anything.

7. You free?
   ······Yes, I am. What do you want?
   Lend us a hand for a moment.

8. Do you have a dictionary?
   ······No, I don't.

Conversation

Shall we go together?

Kobayashi: Are you going home for the summer holidays?
Thawaphon: No, although I'd like to......
Kobayashi: I see.
           Have you ever been up Mount Fuji, Thawaphon?
Thawaphon: No, I haven't.
Kobayashi: How about going together, then?
Thawaphon: OK. When?
Kobayashi: How about the beginning of August?
Thawaphon: Fine.
Kobayashi: OK, I'll check a few things out and give you a call.
Thawaphon: Thanks, I'll be waiting.

20

III. Useful Words and Information

<ruby>人<rt>ひと</rt></ruby>の <ruby>呼<rt>よ</rt></ruby>び<ruby>方<rt>かた</rt></ruby>　　**How to Address People**

"Taro, Hanako!!"

"Darling, it's Taro's birthday today."

In families, people tend to call each other from the viewpoint of the youngest of the family. For example, a parent calls his/her eldest son or daughter おにいちゃん (elder brother) or おねえちゃん (elder sister), standing in the position of his/her younger sister or brother.

When parents talk in the presence of their children, the husband calls his wife おかあさん (Mother) or ママ (Mom), and the wife calls her husband おとうさん (Father) or パパ (Pop). This practice, however, has been changing recently.

"Mr. Matsumoto, could you sign this, please?"

"That suits you very well, Sir (Madam)."

"Doctor, I have a stomachache."

In Japan, people tend to call each other by the names of their role in the group to which they belong. For example, at work, a subordinate calls his boss by his job title. In shops, shop assistants call their customers おきゃくさま (Mr./Ms. Customer). Doctors are called せんせい by their patients.

127

20

IV. Grammar Notes

1. Polite style and plain style

The Japanese language has two styles of speech: polite style and plain style.

Polite style	Plain style
あした 東京_{とうきょう}へ 行_いきます。 I shall be going to Tokyo tomorrow.	あした 東京_{とうきょう}へ 行_いく。 I'm off to Tokyo tomorrow.
毎日_{まいにち} 忙_{いそが}しいです。 I'm busy every day.	毎日_{まいにち} 忙_{いそが}しい。 I'm busy every day.
相撲_{すもう}が 好_すきです。 I like sumo.	相撲_{すもう}が 好_すきだ。 I like sumo.
富士山_{ふじさん}に 登_{のぼ}りたいです。 I'd like to climb Mt Fuji.	富士山_{ふじさん}に 登_{のぼ}りたい。 I want to climb Mt Fuji.
ドイツへ 行_いった ことが ありません。 I've never been to Germany.	ドイツへ 行_いった ことが ない。 I've never been to Germany.

The predicates used in polite-style sentences accompanied by です or ます are called the polite form, while the predicates used in plain-style sentences are called the plain form. （See Exercise A1, Lesson 20 of Main Text.）

128

2. Proper use of the polite style or plain style

1) Conversation

The polite style is used when speaking to a person one has met for the first time, to someone of higher status, and even to people in a similar age group whom one does not know very well.

The plain style is used when talking to one's close friends, colleagues and family members.

Be careful not to use the plain style to the wrong person, as this would be discourteous.

2) Writing

The polite style is commonly used in writing letters, while the plain style is used when writing dissertations, reports, diaries and so on.

3. Conversation in the plain style

1) Questions in the plain style usually omit the particle か from the end, being pronounced with a rising intonation instead, e.g. のむ（↗） or のんだ（↗）.

① コーヒーを 飲_のむ？（↗）　　　Want some coffee?
　……うん、飲_のむ。（↘）　　　……Yeah, sure.

20

2) In noun and な -adj questions, だ (the plain form of です), is omitted. In an answer in the affirmative, ending the sentence with だ could sound a bit harsh, so it is either omitted entirely or replaced by a sentence-ending particle to soften the reply.

② 今晩 暇？ You free tonight?
……うん、暇／暇だ／暇だよ。 ……Yes, I am. (used by men)
……うん、暇／暇よ／暇だよ。 ……Yes, I am. (used by women)
……ううん、暇じゃ ない。 ……No, I'm not.

3) In the plain style, certain particles are often omitted if the meaning of the sentence is evident from the context.

③ ごはん [を] 食べる？ Would you like something to eat?
④ あした 京都 [へ] 行かない？ How about going to Kyoto tomorrow?
⑤ この りんご [は] おいしいね。 These apples are nice, aren't they?
⑥ そこに はさみ [が] ある？ Are there any scissors there?

However, particles like で, に, から, まで and と are not omitted because the meaning of the sentence would be unclear without them.

4) In the plain style, the い of the V て -form いる is also often dropped.

⑦ 辞書、持って [い]る？ Have you got a dictionary?
……うん、持って [い]る。 ……Yes, I have.
……ううん、持って [い]ない。 ……No, I haven't.

5) けど

けど works in the same way as が and is often used in conversation.

⑧ その カレー [は] おいしい？ Is that curry good?
……うん、辛いけど、おいしい。 Yes, it's spicy, but it's nice.
⑨ 相撲の チケット [が] あるけど、いっしょに 行かない？
I've got some tickets for the sumo. Would you like to go with me?
……いいね。 ……That'd be great.

129

20

Lesson 21

I. Vocabulary

おもいますI	思います	think
いいますI	言います	say
かちますI	勝ちます	win
まけますII*	負けます	lose, be beaten
あります I		[a festival] be held, take place
[おまつりが～]	[お祭りが～]	
やくに たちますI	役に 立ちます	be useful
うごきますI	動きます	move, work
やめますII		quit or retire from [a company], stop,
[かいしゃを～]	[会社を～]	give up
きを つけますII	気を つけます	pay attention, take care
りゅうがくしますIII	留学します	study abroad
むだ[な]		wasteful
ふべん[な]	不便[な]	inconvenient
すごい		awful, great（expresses astonishment or admiration）
ほんとう		true
うそ*		lie
じどうしゃ	自動車	car, automobile
こうつう	交通	transport, traffic
ぶっか	物価	[commodity] prices
ほうそう	放送	announcement, broadcast
ニュース		news
アニメ		anime (Japanese animated film)
マンガ		comic book
デザイン		design, artwork
ゆめ	夢	dream
てんさい	天才	genius
しあい	試合	game, match（～を します：play a game/match）

いけん	意見	opinion
はなし	話	talk, speech, what one says, story (〜 を します：talk, tell a story)

ちきゅう	地球	earth
つき	月	moon

さいきん	最近	recently, these days
たぶん		probably, perhaps, maybe
きっと		surely, definitely
ほんとうに		really
そんなに		not so (used with negatives)

〜に ついて		about 〜, concerning 〜

〈会話〉

久しぶりですね。	It's been a long time [since we last met].
〜でも 飲みませんか。	How about drinking 〜 or something?
もちろん	of course
もう 帰らないと……。	I have to get home now......

··

アインシュタイン	Albert Einstein (1879-1955)
ガガーリン	Yuri Alekseyevich Gagarin (1934-1968)
ガリレオ	Galileo Galilei (1564-1642)
キング牧師	Martin Luther King, Jr. (1929-1968)
フランクリン	Benjamin Franklin (1706-1790)
かぐや姫	Princess Kaguya (heroine of the old Japanese folk tale 'Taketori Monogatari')
天神祭	Tenjin Festival (a festival in Osaka)
吉野山	Mt. Yoshino (a mountain in Nara Prefecture)
カンガルー	kangaroo
キャプテン・クック	Captain James Cook (1728-1779)
ヨーネン	a fictitious company

II. Translation

Sentence Patterns

1. I think it's going to rain tomorrow.
2. I told my Dad I want to go abroad to study.
3. I bet you're tired, aren't you?

Example Sentences

1. Where's Mr. Miller?
    ······I think he's probably already gone home.

2. Does Mr. Miller know about this news?
    ······No, I don't think he does.

3. Which is more important, your job or your family?
    ······I think they're both important.

4. What do you think of Japan?
    ······I think the prices are high.

5. Do you say grace before meals?
    ······No, we don't, but we do say, "Itadakimasu".

6. Princess Kaguya said, "I must go back home to the Moon." Then she went back to the Moon. The End.
    ······The End? Mummy, I want to go to the Moon, too.

7. Did you say anything in the meeting?
    ······Yes, I said there was a lot of wasteful copying.

8. There's a festival in Kyoto in July, isn't there?
    ······Yes, there is.

Conversation

I think so, too

Matsumoto:	Hello, Mr. Santos. I haven't seen you for a while, have I?
Santos:	Hi, Mr. Matsumoto. Are you well?
Matsumoto:	Yes, thanks. Shall we go and have for a beer or something?
Santos:	Good idea.

··

Santos:	There's a soccer match between Japan and Brazil at ten o'clock tonight, isn't there?
Matsumoto:	Oh, yes, so there is.
	Which team do you think will win, Mr. Santos?
Santos:	Brazil, of course!
Matsumoto:	Well, maybe. But Japan has also gotten better lately.
Santos:	Yes, I think so, too, but......
	Oh, I have to get home now......
Matsumoto:	Yes, let's go home, shall we?

役職名　Positions in Society
やくしょくめい

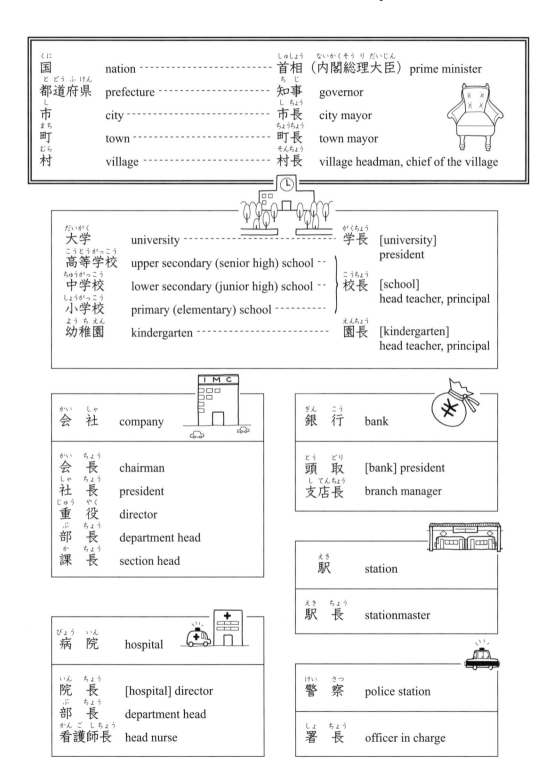

くに国	nation	---------------------------	しゅしょう首相（ないかくそうりだいじん内閣総理大臣）	prime minister
とどうふけん都道府県	prefecture	--------------------	ちじ知事	governor
し市	city	----------------------------	しちょう市長	city mayor
まち町	town	---------------------------	ちょうちょう町長	town mayor
むら村	village	--------------------	そんちょう村長	village headman, chief of the village

だいがく大学	university	------------------------	がくちょう学長	[university] president
こうとうがっこう高等学校	upper secondary (senior high) school	--		
ちゅうがっこう中学校	lower secondary (junior high) school	--	こうちょう校長	[school] head teacher, principal
しょうがっこう小学校	primary (elementary) school	---------		
ようちえん幼稚園	kindergarten	----------------------	えんちょう園長	[kindergarten] head teacher, principal

133

かいしゃ会社	company
かいちょう会長	chairman
しゃちょう社長	president
じゅうやく重役	director
ぶちょう部長	department head
かちょう課長	section head

ぎんこう銀行	bank
とうどり頭取	[bank] president
してんちょう支店長	branch manager

| えき駅 | station |
| えきちょう駅長 | stationmaster |

びょういん病院	hospital
いんちょう院長	[hospital] director
ぶちょう部長	department head
かんごしちょう看護師長	head nurse

| けいさつ警察 | police station |
| しょちょう署長 | officer in charge |

IV. Grammar Notes

1. | **Plain form と 思^{おも}います** | I think that......

The ideas or judgements expressed with おもいますare indicated by the particle と.
This sentence pattern is used in the following ways:

1) When expressing conjecture

① あした 雨^{あめ}が 降^ふると 思^{おも}います。　I think it's going to rain tomorrow.

② テレーザちゃんは もう 寝^ねたと 思^{おも}います。
I think Teresa's already gone to bed.

To express a negative conjecture, the clause before と is put in the negative.

③ ミラーさんは この ニュースを 知^しって いますか。
……いいえ、知^しらないと 思^{おも}います。
Has Mr. Miller heard that news?
……No, I don't think he has.

2) When stating an opinion

④ 日本^{にほん}は 物価^{ぶっか}が 高^{たか}いと 思^{おも}います。　I think that prices in Japan are high.

When asking someone's opinion about something, the expression ～に ついて どう おもいますか is used, without putting と after the どう.

⑤ 新^{あたら}しい 空港^{くうこう}に ついて どう 思^{おも}いますか。
……きれいですが、ちょっと 交通^{こうつう}が 不便^{ふべん}だと 思^{おも}います。
What do you think of the new airport?
……I think it's lovely, but it's a bit hard to get to.

Agreement with someone else's opinion is expressed like this:

⑥ ケータイは 便利^{べんり}ですね。　　Mobile phones are handy, aren't they?
……わたしも そう 思^{おも}います。　……Yes, I think so, too.

2. | **"Sentences"　Plain form** } と 言^いいます | say......

The particle と is used to report speech. There are two ways of doing this:

1) When reporting speech directly, it is repeated word for word. In writing, the words are placed inside square brackets「 」.

⑦ 寝^ねる まえに、「お休^{やす}みなさい」と 言^いいます。
We say, "Good night" before going to bed.

⑧ ミラーさんは「来週^{らいしゅう} 東京^{とうきょう}へ 出張^{しゅっちょう}します」と 言^いいました。
Mr. Miller said, "I'm going to Tokyo on business next week."

2) When reporting speech indirectly, the plain form is used before と.

⑨ ミラーさんは 東京^{とうきょう}へ 出張^{しゅっちょう}すると 言^いいました。
Mr. Miller said that he would be going to Tokyo on business.

The tense of the quoted sentence is not affected by the tense of the main sentence.

The particle に is used to indicate the person spoken to.

⑩ 父に 留学したいと 言いました。

I told my father that I wanted to study abroad.

3.

V		plain form		でしょう？	......right?
い -adj		plain form			
な -adj		plain form			
N		～だ			

This sentence form is used when seeking agreement or confirmation from the listener.
でしょう is spoken with a rising intonation.

The plain form is used before でしょう, but without the ～だ in the case of a な -adj or noun.

⑪ あした パーティーに 行くでしょう？

You're going to the party tomorrow, right?

……ええ、行きます。   ……Yes, I am.

⑫ 北海道は 寒かったでしょう？   I bet it was cold in Hokkaido, wasn't it?

……いいえ、そんなに 寒くなかったです。

……No, it wasn't so cold.

4. $\boxed{\text{N}_1(\text{place}) で \text{N}_2 が あります}$

When N₂ is a ceremony or event such as a party, concert, festival, incident or disaster, あります is used in the sense of 'to take place', 'to be held' or 'to occur'.

⑬ 東京で 日本と ブラジルの サッカーの 試合が あります。

There's a soccer match between Japan and Brazil in Tokyo.

5. $\boxed{\text{N}(\text{occasion}) で}$

The occasion at which an action takes place is marked by で.

⑭ 会議で 何か 意見を 言いましたか。   Did you say anything at the meeting?

6. $\boxed{\text{N でも V}}$

When recommending, suggesting, or expressing a hope for something, the particle でも is used to give an example, without restricting it to a specific one.

⑮ ちょっと ビールでも 飲みませんか。 How about drinking a beer or something?

7. $\boxed{\text{V ない -form ないと……}}$

This expression is created by omitting the いけません from V ない -form ないと いけません (see Lesson 17). Vない-formないと いけません means more or less the same as Vない -form なければ なりません, which was presented in Lesson 17.

⑯ もう 帰らないと……。   I have to be getting home......

Lesson 22

I. Vocabulary

きますⅡ	着ます	put on (a shirt, etc.)
はきますⅠ		put on (shoes, trousers, etc.)
かぶりますⅠ		put on (a hat, etc.)
かけますⅡ		put on [glasses]
［めがねを～］	［眼鏡を～］	
しますⅢ		put on [tie]
［ネクタイを～］		
うまれますⅡ	生まれます	be born
わたしたち		we
コート		coat
セーター		sweater
スーツ *		suit
ぼうし	帽子	hat, cap
めがね	眼鏡	glasses
ケーキ		cake
［お］べんとう	［お］弁当	box lunch
ロボット		robot
ユーモア		humor
つごう	都合	convenience
よく		often

〈練習 C〉

えーと	well, let me see
おめでとう［ございます］。	Congratulations.（used on birthdays, at weddings, New Year's Day, etc.）

〈会話〉

お探しですか。	Are you looking for 〜?
では	Well then,
こちら	this（polite equivalent of これ）
家賃	rent
ダイニングキッチン	kitchen with a dining area
和室	Japanese-style room
押し入れ	Japanese-style closet
布団	Japanese-style mattress and quilt

....

パリ	Paris
万里の長城	the Great Wall of China
みんなの アンケート	title of a fictitious questionnaire

II. Translation

Sentence Patterns

1. This cake was made by Mr. Miller.
2. That person over there is Mr. Miller.
3. I've forgotten the words I learnt yesterday.
4. I don't have time to go shopping.

Example Sentences

1. These are some photographs I took at the Great Wall of China.
   ......Really? Amazing, isn't it?

2. Which is the painting that Karina did?
   ......That one. That painting of the sea.

3. Who's that person wearing a kimono?
   ......That's Ms. Kimura.

4. Mr. Yamada, where did you first meet your wife?
   ......At Osaka Castle.

5. How was the concert you went to with Ms. Kimura?
   ......It was very good.

6. What's the matter?
   ......I've lost the umbrella I bought yesterday.

7. What kind of house do you want?
   ......I want a house with a big garden.

8. Would you like to go and watch the soccer on Sunday?
   ......Sorry, I've promised to meet some friends on Sunday.

Conversation

What kind of flat are you looking for?

Letting agent:	What kind of flat are you looking for?
Wang:	Let me see......
	A place where the rent is about eighty thousand yen, not far from the station, would be good.
Letting agent:	How about this one, then?
	It's ten minutes from the station, and the rent is eighty-three thousand yen.
Wang:	It's got an eat-in kitchen and one Japanese-style room, right?
	Excuse me. What's this?
Letting agent:	That's an 'oshiire'. It's a place to put a futon in.
Wang:	I see.
	Can I see this flat today?
Letting agent:	Yes. Shall we go now?
Wang:	Yes, please.

III. Useful Words and Information

衣服　Clothes

スーツ suit	ワンピース one-piece dress	上着 jacket	ズボン／パンツ trousers/pants ジーンズ jeans
スカート skirt	ブラウス blouse	ワイシャツ [white] shirt	セーター sweater
マフラー scarf, muffler 手袋　gloves	下着 underwear	くつした　socks （パンティー） ストッキング tights, panty hose	着物　kimono 帯　obi
（オーバー）コート overcoat レインコート raincoat	ネクタイ tie, necktie ベルト　belt	ハイヒール high heels ブーツ boots 運動靴 trainers, sneakers	ぞうり　　たび zori　　tabi

IV. Grammar Notes

1. Noun modification

Lessons 2 and 8 explained how to modify nouns.

ミラーさんの うち	Mr. Miller's house (See Lesson 2.)
新しい うち	a new house (See Lesson 8.)
きれいな うち	a beautiful house (See Lesson 8.)

The modifying word or clause comes before the noun. This lesson explains how to use a clause to modify a noun.

1) Verbs, adjectives and nouns in a clause that modifies a noun are in the plain form. With な -adjectives, this is 〜な, and with nouns it is 〜の.

① 京都へ	行く 人	a person who goes to Kyoto
	行かない 人	a person who does not go to Kyoto
	行った 人	a person who went to Kyoto
	行かなかった 人	a person who did not go to Kyoto
背が 高くて、髪が 黒い 人		a tall, black-haired person
親切で、きれいな 人		a beautiful, kind person
65歳の 人		a 65-year-old person

2) Noun-modifying clauses are used with the various sentence patterns illustrated below.

② これは ミラーさんが 住んで いた うちです。
This is the house where Mr. Miller used to live.

③ ミラーさんが 住んで いた うちは 古いです。
The house where Mr. Miller used to live is old.

④ ミラーさんが 住んで いた うちを 買いました。
I bought the house where Mr. Miller used to live.

⑤ わたしは ミラーさんが 住んで いた うちが 好きです。
I like the house where Mr. Miller used to live.

⑥ ミラーさんが 住んで いた うちに 猫が いました。
There was a cat in the house where Mr. Miller used to live.

⑦ ミラーさんが 住んで いた うちへ 行った ことが あります。
I've been to the house where Mr. Miller used to live.

3）The subject of a noun-modifying clause is marked by が.

⑧　これは　ミラーさんが　作った　ケーキです。

This cake was baked by Mr. Miller.

⑨　わたしは　カリナさんが　かいた　絵が　好きです。

I like the picture that Karina painted.

⑩　[あなたは]　彼が　生まれた　所を　知って　いますか。

Do you know the place where he was born?

2. | V-dictionary form 時間／約束／用事 |

When talking about the time required for doing something or describing an appointment, errand, etc., the verb is put in the dictionary form and is placed in front of the noun じかん, やくそく, ようじ, etc.

⑪　わたしは　朝ごはんを　食べる　時間が　ありません。

I don't have time to eat breakfast.

⑫　わたしは　友達と　映画を　見る　約束が　あります。

I've arranged to see a film with some friends.

⑬　きょうは　市役所へ　行く　用事が　あります。

I have to do something at City Hall today.

3. | V ます -form ましょうか | Shall we......?

This sentence pattern was presented in Lesson 14 as an expression for when the speaker is offering to do something for the listener. However, in this Lesson's Conversation, it is presented as an expression for when the speaker is suggesting to the listener that they do something together.

⑭　この　部屋、きょう　見る　ことが　できますか。　　Can I see this flat today?
　　……ええ。今から　行きましょうか。　　……Yes. Shall we go now?

Lesson 23

I. Vocabulary

ききますⅠ 　[せんせいに〜]	聞きます 　[先生に〜]	ask [the teacher]
まわしますⅠ	回します	turn
ひきますⅠ	引きます	pull
かえますⅡ	変えます	change
さわりますⅠ 　[ドアに〜]	触ります	touch [a door]
でますⅡ[おつりが〜]	出ます[お釣りが〜]	[change] come out
あるきますⅠ	歩きます	walk
わたりますⅠ 　[はしを〜]	渡ります 　[橋を〜]	cross [a bridge]
まがりますⅠ 　[みぎへ〜]	曲がります 　[右へ〜]	turn [to the right]
さびしい	寂しい	lonely
［お］ゆ	［お］湯	hot water
おと	音	sound
サイズ		size
こしょう	故障	breakdown（〜します：break down）
みち	道	road, way
こうさてん	交差点	crossroads
しんごう	信号	traffic lights
かど	角	corner
はし	橋	bridge
ちゅうしゃじょう	駐車場	car park, parking lot
たてもの	建物	building
なんかいも	何回も	many times
ーめ	ー目	the -th（indicating order）

聖徳太子 Prince Shotoku (574-622)
しょうとくたいし

法隆寺 Horyuji Temple, a temple in Nara
ほうりゅうじ Prefecture built by Prince Shotoku
at the beginning of the 7th century

元気茶 a fictitious tea
げんきちゃ

本田駅 a fictitious station
ほんだえき

図書館前 a fictitious bus stop
としょかんまえ

23

II. Translation

Sentence Patterns

1. When you borrow a book from the library, you need your card.
2. If you press this button, your change comes out.

Example Sentences

1. Do you watch much TV?
   ……Well, I usually watch baseball games when they're on.

2. What do you do when there's nothing in the fridge?
   ……I go and eat in a nearby restaurant.

3. Did you switch off the air conditioner when you left the meeting room?
   ……Yes, I did.

4. Where do you buy your clothes and shoes, Mr. Santos?
   ……I buy them when I go back to my own country, because Japanese ones are too small.

5. What's that?
   ……It's 'Genki-cha'. I drink it when I don't feel very well.

6. Won't you come and visit us when you have some time to spare?
   ……Yes, I will. Thank you.

7. Did you have any part-time jobs when you were at university?
   ……Yes, sometimes.

8. There's no hot water coming out.
   ……It'll come out if you press there.

9. Excuse me, where's the city hall?
   ……Go straight down this street, and it's on the left. It's an old building.

Conversation

How do you get there?

Librarian: Hello, Midori Library.

Karina: Can you tell me how to get to you, please?

Librarian: Get on the number twelve bus at Honda station and get off at Toshokanmae.
It's the third stop.

Karina: The third stop, right?

Librarian: Yes, when you get off, you'll see a park in front of you.
The library is the white building in the park.

Karina: I see.
And what do I need to bring with me to take out a book?

Librarian: Please bring something that shows your name and address.

Karina: OK. Thank you very much.

III. Useful Words and Information

道路・交通　Roads and Traffic

① 歩道　　　　　　pavement, sidewalk
② 車道　　　　　　road
③ 高速道路　　　　motorway, expressway
④ 通り　　　　　　street
⑤ 交差点　　　　　crossing
⑥ 横断歩道　　　　pedestrian crossing
⑦ 歩道橋　　　　　pedestrian bridge
⑧ 角　　　　　　　corner

⑨ 信号　　　　　　traffic light
⑩ 坂　　　　　　　slope
⑪ 踏切　　　　　　railway crossing
⑫ ガソリンスタンド　petrol station, gas station

止まれ	進入禁止	一方通行	駐車禁止	右折禁止
Stop	No Entry	One Way	No Parking	No Right Turn

IV. Grammar Notes

1.

| V-dictionary form
V ない -form ない
い -adj(〜い)
な -adj な
N の | とき、〜(main clause) | When...... |

とき is used to connects two sentences while expressing a time or occasion when the state or action described in the main sentence exists or occurs. The form of the word preceding とき is the same as the form that modifies a noun.

① 図書館で 本を 借りる とき、カードが 要ります。

You need your card when you borrow a book from the library.

② 使い方が わからない とき、わたしに 聞いて ください。

If you don't know how to use it, please ask me.

③ 体の 調子が 悪い とき、「元気茶」を 飲みます。

When I don't feel very well, I drink 'Genki-cha'.

④ 暇な とき、うちへ 遊びに 来ませんか。

Please come and visit me when you have some free time.

⑤ 妻が 病気の とき、会社を 休みます。

I take time off when my wife is ill.

⑥ 若い とき、あまり 勉強しませんでした。

I didn't study very much when I was young.

⑦ 子どもの とき、よく 川で 泳ぎました。

I often swam in the river when I was a child.

The tense of the clause modifying とき is not affected by the tense of the main clause.

2.

| V-dictionary form
V た -form | とき、〜(main clause) | When...... |

When the verb in front of とき is in the dictionary form, whatever is described in the main clause happened before whatever is described in the 〜とき clause. When the verb in front of とき is in the た -form, whatever is described in the main clause happened after whatever is described in the 〜とき clause.

⑧ パリへ 行く とき、かばんを 買いました。

I bought a bag when going to Paris.

⑨ パリへ 行った とき、かばんを 買いました。

I bought a bag when I went to Paris.

⑧ means that the bag was bought before arriving in Paris, i.e. it was bought on the way there, while ⑨ means that the bag was bought after arriving in Paris, i.e. it was bought in Paris.

3. V-dictionary form と、～(main clause)   If ...... then ......

This sentence pattern is used to indicate that if a certain action, situation or phenomenon (the one before と) occurs, then another action, situation or phenomenon (the one in the main clause, after と) will incvitably occur.

⑩ この ボタンを 押すと、お釣りが 出ます。
   If you press this button, you'll get your change.

⑪ これを 回すと、音が 大きく なります。
   When you turn this, it gets louder.

⑫ 右へ 曲がると、郵便局が あります。
   If you turn right, you'll see a post office.

4. N が adj

It was explained in Lesson 14 that が is used when describing a phenomenon in terms of how it was perceived with the five senses (sight, hearing, etc.) or when objectively reporting an event. が can be used not only with verb sentences but also with adjective sentences.

⑬ 音が 小さいです。   The volume is low.

5. N を motionV

を is used with motion verbs such as さんぽします, わたります and あるきます to indicate the place that people or things pass through.

⑭ 公園を 散歩します。   I go for a walk in the park. (See Lesson 13.)

⑮ 道を 渡ります。   I cross the road.

⑯ 交差点を 右へ 曲がります。   I turn right at the intersection.

Lesson 24

I. Vocabulary

くれますⅡ		give (me)
なおしますⅠ	直します	repair, correct
つれて いきますⅠ	連れて 行きます	take (someone)
つれて きますⅢ＊	連れて 来ます	bring (someone)
おくりますⅠ	送ります	escort [someone], go with
［ひとを～］	［人を～］	
しょうかいしますⅢ	紹介します	introduce
あんないしますⅢ	案内します	show around, show the way
せつめいしますⅢ	説明します	explain
おじいさん／		grandfather, old man
おじいちゃん		
おばあさん／		grandmother, old woman
おばあちゃん		
じゅんび	準備	preparation（～[を] します：prepare）
ひっこし	引っ越し	moving out（～[を] します：move out）
［お］かし	［お］菓子	sweets, snacks
ホームステイ		homestay
ぜんぶ	全部	all
じぶんで	自分で	by oneself

〈会話〉

ほかに   besides

....

母の日   Mother's Day

II. Translation

Sentence Patterns

1. Ms. Sato gave me some chocolate.
2. Mr. Yamada corrected my report for me.
3. My mother sent me a sweater.
4. I lent Ms. Kimura a book.

Example Sentences

1. Do you love Granny, Taro?
   ⋯⋯Yes, I do. She always gives me sweet things to eat.

2. Nice wine, isn't it?
   ⋯⋯Yes, Ms. Sato gave it to me. It's French.

3. Mr. Miller, did you cook all the food at yesterday's party yourself?
   ⋯⋯No, Mr. Wang helped me.

4. Did you go by train?
   ⋯⋯No, Mr. Yamada took me in his car.

5. Taro, what are you going to do for your mother on Mother's Day?
   ⋯⋯I'm going to play the piano for her.

Conversation

Shall I come and help?

Karina: Mr. Wang, you're moving on Sunday, aren't you?
Shall I come and help?

Wang: Thank you.
OK then, if you don't mind, please come at about nine o'clock.

Karina: Is anyone else coming to help?

Wang: Mr. Yamada and Mr. Miller are coming.

Karina: What about a car?

Wang: Mr. Yamada is lending me his.

Karina: What are you doing about lunch?

Wang: Er⋯⋯

Karina: Shall I bring a packed lunch?

Wang. Yes, please. Thanks.

Karina: See you on Sunday then.

III. Useful Words and Information

<ruby>贈答<rt>ぞうとう</rt></ruby>の <ruby>習慣<rt>しゅうかん</rt></ruby>　　**Exchanging Gifts**

お<ruby>年玉<rt>としだま</rt></ruby>	Small gift of money given by parents and relatives to children on New Year's Day
<ruby>入学<rt>にゅうがく</rt></ruby><ruby>祝<rt>いわ</rt></ruby>い	Gift celebrating admission to school (money, stationery, book, etc.)
<ruby>卒業<rt>そつぎょう</rt></ruby><ruby>祝<rt>いわ</rt></ruby>い	Graduation gift (money, stationery, book, etc.)
<ruby>結婚<rt>けっこん</rt></ruby><ruby>祝<rt>いわ</rt></ruby>い	Wedding gift (money, household goods, etc.)
<ruby>出産<rt>しゅっさん</rt></ruby><ruby>祝<rt>いわ</rt></ruby>い	Gift celebrating a birth (baby clothes, toys, etc.)

お<ruby>中元<rt>ちゅうげん</rt></ruby> [Jul. or Aug.]
お<ruby>歳暮<rt>せいぼ</rt></ruby> [Dec.]
} Gift for a person whose care you are under, e.g., doctor, teacher, boss, etc. (food, etc.)

お<ruby>香典<rt>こうでん</rt></ruby>	Condolence money
お<ruby>見舞<rt>みま</rt></ruby>い	Present given when visiting a sick or injured person (flowers, fruit, etc.)

151

 <ruby>熨斗袋<rt>のしぶくろ</rt></ruby> **Special decorated envelope for money gifts**
The right envelope for the occasion should be used.

For weddings (with red and white, or gold and silver ribbon)

For celebrations other than weddings (with red and white, or gold and silver ribbon)

For funerals (with black and white ribbon)

IV. Grammar Notes

1. くれます

The word あげます (give), which was taught in Lesson 7, cannot be used to talk about someone else giving something to the speaker or a member of his or her family. In that case, the word くれます is used.

① わたしは 佐藤さんに 花を あげました。

I gave some flowers to Ms. Sato.

×佐藤さんは わたしに クリスマスカードを あげました。

② 佐藤さんは わたしに クリスマスカードを くれました。

Ms. Sato gave me a Christmas card.

③ 佐藤さんは 妹に お菓子を くれました。

Ms. Sato gave some candies to my younger sister.

2.

V て -form	あげます
	もらいます
	くれます

あげます, もらいます and くれます refer to the giving and receiving of things, while 〜て あげます, 〜て もらいます and 〜て くれます are used to denote that an action confers some kind of profit or benefit on the recipient.

1) | V て -form あげます |

The pattern verb て -form あげます is used when the person doing the action is taken as the subject. It shows that the action confers some kind of profit or benefit on the recipient.

④ わたしは 木村さんに 本を 貸して あげました。

I lent Ms. Kimura a book.

Because the 〜て あげます pattern denotes the conferral of some kind of profit or benefit, it could sound patronizing if used when the recipient is of higher status than the person conferring the profit or benefit. It is better in this case to use the pattern verb ます -form ましょうか (see Lesson 14-5).

⑤ タクシーを 呼びましょうか。

Shall I call a cab? (See Lesson 14.)

⑥ 手伝いましょうか。

May I help you? (See Lesson 14.)

2) | V て -form もらいます |

⑦ わたしは 山田さんに 図書館の 電話番号を 教えて もらいました。

Mr. Yamada told me the telephone number of the library.

This shows that the speaker feels that the person for whom the action was performed (who is taken as the subject of this sentence) has received some profit or benefit from

24

152

the action. When the subject is わたし, it is usually omitted.

3) | Verb て -form くれます |

⑧ 母は [わたしに] セーターを 送って くれました。

My mother sent me a sweater.

Here, the person performing the action is taken as the subject, and the form shows that the speaker feels that the person for whom the action was performed has benefited from the action. When the person benefiting from the action (marked by the particle に) is わたし, it is usually omitted.

[Note] In a sentence using ～て あげます or ～て くれます, the particle that marks the person receiving the benefit is the same as in an equivalent sentence that does not use ～て あげます or ～て くれます.

わたしに 旅行の 写真を 見せます。
↓
わたしに 旅行の 写真を 見せて くれます。

He shows me the photos taken during the travel.

わたしを 大阪城へ 連れて 行きます。
↓
わたしを 大阪城へ 連れて 行って くれます。

He takes me to Osaka Castle.

わたしの 引っ越しを 手伝います。
↓
わたしの 引っ越しを 手伝って くれます。

He helps me move.

3. | N₁ は N₂ が V |

⑨ おいしい ワインですね。

……ええ、[この ワインは] 佐藤さんが くれました。

This wine is very nice, isn't it?

……Yes, Ms. Sato gave it to me.

The response to this question takes as its topic the object of the sentence さとうさんが この ワインを くれました, i.e. この ワインを (see Lesson 17-5). Since この ワインは is understood by both the speaker and the listener, it can be omitted. As the subject of this sentence is さとうさん, it is marked by が.

Lesson 25

I. Vocabulary

かんがえます II	考えます	think, consider
つきます I	着きます	arrive
とります I	取ります	grow old
［としを～］	［年を～］	
たります II	足ります	be enough, be sufficient
いなか	田舎	countryside, hometown
チャンス		chance
おく	億	hundred million
もし ［～たら］		if
いみ	意味	meaning

<練習 C>
もしもし   hello（used on the phone）

<会話>
転勤   transter（〜します：be transferred to another office）

こと   thing, matter（〜の こと：thing about 〜）

暇   free time

［いろいろ］お世話に なりました。   Thank you for everything you've done for me.

頑張ります I   do one's best

どうぞ お元気で。   Please take care of youreslf.（said when expecting a long separation）

ベトナム   Vietnam

II. Translation

Sentence Patterns
1. I'm not going out if it rains.
2. I'm going out even if it rains.

Example Sentences
1. What would you like to do if you had a hundred million yen?
    ⋯⋯ I'd like to build a school.

2. What will you do if there aren't any trains or buses running?
    ⋯⋯ I'll walk home.

3. That new shoe shop has a lot of nice shoes, you know.
    ⋯⋯ Really? I'd like to buy a pair if they're cheap enough.

4. Do I have to come tomorrow, too?
    ⋯⋯ No, if you can't make it, please come next week.

5. Have you thought of a name for the baby yet?
    ⋯⋯ Yes, Hikaru if it's a boy, and Aya if it's a girl.

6. Are you going to get a job as soon as you've left university?
    ⋯⋯ No, I want to go travelling around the world for a year or so.

7. Miss, I don't know what this word means.
    ⋯⋯ Did you look it up in the dictionary?
    Yes, but I still don't understand it.

8. Do you put the air conditioner on when it's hot?
    ⋯⋯ No, I don't put it on even if it's hot. I don't think it's good for one's health.

Conversation
Thanks for everything

Kimura: Congratulations on your move.

Miller: Thank you.

Kimura: We'll miss you, Mr. Miller when you've gone to Tokyo, won't we?

Sato: Yes, we will.

Kimura: Even after you've gone to Tokyo, please don't forget Osaka, will you?

Miller: Of course not. Everybody, when you have some spare time, please be sure to come and visit me in Tokyo.

Santos: And you please call us if you come to Osaka, Mr. Miller, and let's go out for a drink together.

Miller: Yes, definitely.
Everybody, I'm really grateful for everything you've done for me.

Sato: Good luck, and look after yourself.

Miller: Yes, I will. And all of you take care, too.

III. Useful Words and Information

ひと いっしょう
人の 一生　　Life

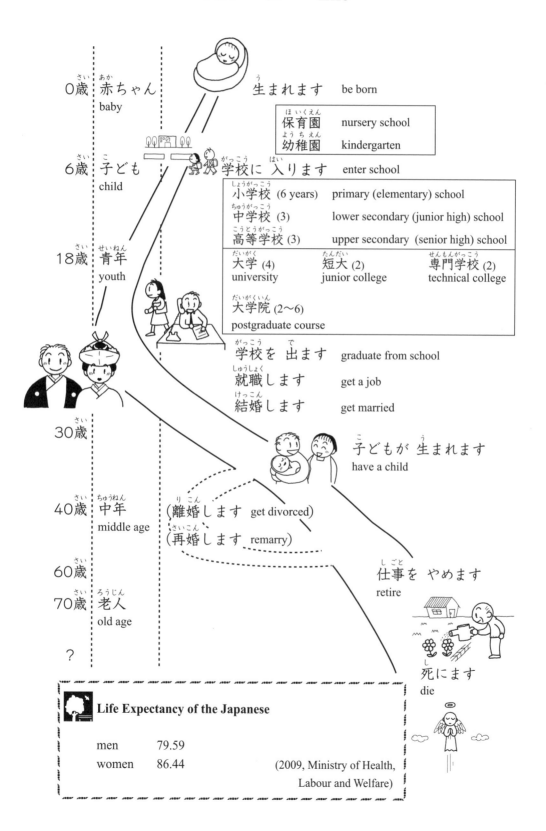

0歳 赤ちゃん
baby

生まれます　be born

保育園　nursery school
幼稚園　kindergarten

6歳 子ども　学校に 入ります　enter school
child

小学校 (6 years)　primary (elementary) school
中学校 (3)　lower secondary (junior high) school
高等学校 (3)　upper secondary (senior high) school

大学 (4)　短大 (2)　専門学校 (2)
university　junior college　technical college

大学院 (2〜6)
postgraduate course

18歳 青年
youth

学校を 出ます　graduate from school
就職します　get a job
結婚します　get married

子どもが 生まれます
have a child

30歳

40歳 中年
middle age

(離婚します　get divorced)
(再婚します　remarry)

60歳

仕事を やめます
retire

70歳 老人
old age

?

死にます
die

Life Expectancy of the Japanese

men　　79.59
women　86.44

(2009, Ministry of Health,
Labour and Welfare)

IV. Grammar Notes

1. | **Plain past form** ら、～**(main clause)** | If......

Attaching ら to the past-tense plain form of verbs, adjectives, or nouns, makes there conditional. The clause that follows it (the main clause) describes what will happen if the conditional clause were true. The speaker's opinion, wishes, invitations, requests, etc. can be expressed in the main clause.

① お金が あったら、旅行します。

I'd I had some money, I'd go travelling.

② 時間が なかったら、テレビを 見ません。

If I don't have time, I won't watch TV.

③ 安かったら、パソコンを 買いたいです。

I'd like to buy a PC if I can find a cheap one.

④ 暇だったら、手伝って ください。

Please lend me a hand if you're free.

⑤ いい 天気だったら、散歩しませんか。

Shall we go for a walk if the weather's nice?

[Note] Expressions of wish, desire, invitation, request and so on cannot be used in a clause (the main clause) following ～と .

×時間が あると、┌ コンサートに 行きます。　　　(intention)
　　　　　　　├ コンサートに 行きたいです。　(wish)
　　　　　　　├ コンサートに 行きませんか。　(invitation)
　　　　　　　└ ちょっと 手伝って ください。(request)

2. | **V た -form** ら、～**(main clause)** | When....../After....../Once......

This pattern is used to express that a certain action will be done or a certain situation will arise on the completion or occurrence of a matter, action or state that the speaker is certain will happen.

⑥ 10時に なったら、出かけましょう。

Shall we go out once it gets to 10 o'clock?

⑦ うちへ 帰ったら、すぐ シャワーを 浴びます。

I take a shower as soon as I get home.

25

158

3.

V て -form V ない -form なくて い -adj (〜ϊ) → 〜くて な -adj [な] → 〜で N で	も、〜(main clause)	Even if......

This expression is used to present contrasting conditions. The clause that follows て-form も (the main clause) describes something that will happen that would not normally be expected to happen if what was stated in the main clause were true.

⑧ 雨が 降っても、洗濯します。　　I'll do the laundry even if it rains.

⑨ 安くても、わたしは グループ旅行が 嫌いです。

I hate package holidays, even if they are cheap.

⑩ 便利でも、パソコンを 使いません。

I'm not going to use a PC, even if it is convenient.

⑪ 日曜日でも、働きます。　　　I'm going to work, even if it is Sunday.

4. | もし |

もし is used in conjunction with 〜たら to give notice that the clause following it is conditional. It intensifies the speaker's sense of conditionality.

⑫ もし 1億円 あったら、いろいろな 国を 旅行したいです。

If I had a hundred million yen, I'd like to travel round the world.

5. Subject of a subordinate clause

It was explained in Lesson 16-2 that the subject of the clause 〜てから is marked by が. In the same way as 〜てから, 〜とき, 〜と, 〜まえに, etc., the subject of a subordinate clause containing 〜たら or 〜ても is also marked by が.

⑬ 友達が 来る まえに、部屋を 掃除します。

I'm going to clean up my room before my friends arrive. (See Lesson 18.)

⑭ 妻が 病気の とき、会社を 休みます。

I take time off when my wife is ill. (See Lesson 23.)

⑮ 友達が 約束の 時間に 来なかったら、どう しますか。

What will you do if your friends don't arrive at the agreed time? (See Lesson 25.)

Article 1: Topic and Subject

··

1. What is a Topic?

Most Japanese sentences have a topic. The topic appears at the head of the sentence and indicates what is being discussed in the sentence. Sentence (1) below, for example, establishes 東京 as the topic and then discusses it, stating that it is 日本の 首都.

(1) 東京は 日本の 首都です。　Tokyo is the capital of Japan.

Similarly, sentences (2) and (3) below discuss the topics この 部屋 and わたし respectively.

(2) この 部屋は 静かです。　This room is quiet.

(3) わたしは 先週 ディズニーランドへ 行きました。

I went to Disneyland last week.

The topic of a sentence is marked by the particle は. This means that a sentence with a topic is composed of two main parts, one before the は (the topic) and the other after it (the discourse).

(1) 東京は 日本の 首都です。
　　 topic　　　　 discourse

2. What is a Subject?

The subject of a sentence is the most important element for the sentence's predicate (a verb, adjective or noun ＋ です). For example, with verbs such as 飲みます (drink) or 走ります (run), the subject is whoever is doing the drinking or running; with verbs such as います or あります (be, exist), it is the person or thing that exists; with verbs such as 降ります (rain) or 吹きます (blow) it is the event's principal actor (i.e. whatever is raining or blowing); with adjectives such as 大きいです (big) or 有名です (famous) or nouns such as 学生です (student) or 病気です (illness), it is the possessor of the attribute mentioned; and with adjectival predicates such as 好きです (like) or 怖いです (fear), it is the experiencer of the feeling mentioned. Thus, all of the noun phrases underlined in the examples below are subjects.

In sentences that do not have a topic, the subject is marked by the particle が.

(4) 太郎が ビールを 飲みました。　Taro drank some beer.

(5) 机の 上に 本が あります。　There is a book on the desk.

(6) きのう　雨が　降りました。　　It rained yesterday.

3. How Do Topics and Subjects Relate to Each Other?

Although topics and subjects are different concepts, they are closely related. In most sentences with a topic, the topic is also the subject. For example, 田中さん, 佐藤さん and わたし in sentences (7), (8) and (9) below are all topics (because they are all marked with は), but at the same time they are also subjects (because they are each the possessor of an attribute or the experiencer of a feeling).

(7) 田中さんは　有名です。　　Mr. Tanaka is famous.

(8) 佐藤さんは　学生です。　　Ms. Sato is a student.

(9) わたしは　犬が　怖いです。　　I'm scared of dogs.

Although it is relatively common for the topic and subject of a sentence to coincide like this, sometimes they do not. In sentence (10) below, for example, この　本 is the topic (because it is marked with は), but (because it is 田中さん who performs the action of 書きます) この　本 is not the subject.

(10) この　本は　田中さんが　書きました。　　Mr. Tanaka wrote this book.

Sentence (10) can be thought of as being sentence (11) with この　本を taken as the topic.

(11) 田中さんが　この　本を　書きました。　　Mr. Tanaka wrote this book.

(12) この　本をは　田中さんが　書きました。　　Mr. Tanaka wrote this book.

In other words, この　本 has moved to the head of the sentence, and is marked with は to indicate that it is the topic. However, because を and は cannot be used together when this is done, を is eliminated and only は remains, forming sentence (10).

Note that, although が and を cannot be combined with は, other particles can, so sentences like (13) and (14) are possible.

(13) 田中さんには　わたしが　連絡します。

I will get in touch with Mr. Tanaka.

(14) 山田さんからは　返事が　来ませんでした。

No reply came from Ms. Yamada.

4. Sentences with and without Topics

Although most Japanese sentences have topics, some do not. In a sentence with a topic, the subject is marked by は, and in a sentence without a topic, it is marked by

が. Some examples of the use of topic-less sentences are given below.

1) When describing an event exactly as seen, heard, etc.

A sentence without a topic is used when describing an event exactly as perceived by any of the five senses:

(15) あっ、雨が 降って います。　Oh, it's raining.

(16) ラジオの 音が 小さいです。　The radio's [too] quiet.

(17) (窓の 外を 見て) 月が きれいだなぁ。

(*looking out of a window*) The moon's lovely, isn't it?

2) When communicating an event objectively, or at the start of a story

A topic-less sentence is also used in these cases:

(18) きのう 太郎が 来ました。　Taro came yesterday.

(19) 来週 パーティーが あります。　There's a party next week.

(20) むかしむかし ある ところに おじいさんと おばあさんが いました。

Long, long ago, in a certain place, there was an old man and an old woman.

Article 2: **Clauses**

··

A clause is the form that a sentence takes when it is part of a longer sentence.

For example, in (1) and (2) below, the sentences 田中さんが ここへ 来ました and あした 雨が 降ります have become part of a longer sentence, taking the underlined forms.

(1) 田中さんが ここへ 来た とき、山田さんは いませんでした。

　　When Ms. Tanaka arrived, Mr. Yamada wasn't here.

(2) あした 雨が 降ったら、わたしは 出かけません。

　　If it rains tomorrow, I'm not going out.

A clause that forms part of a longer sentence in this way is called a subordinate clause, while the part of the sentence left behind if the subordinate clause is removed is called the main clause.

A subordinate clause amplifies the meaning of the main clause. For example, the subordinate clause in example (2) limits what is said in the main clause by specifying あした 雨が 降ったら as a condition of my not going out.

In Japanese, a subordinate clause usually precedes the main clause.

The subject of a subordinate clause is marked by が, not by は, except when the clause is a 〜が or a 〜けど clauses.

APPENDICES

I. Numerals

0	ゼロ、れい	100	ひゃく
1	いち	200	にひゃく
2	に	300	さんびゃく
3	さん	400	よんひゃく
4	よん、し	500	ごひゃく
5	ご	600	ろっぴゃく
6	ろく	700	ななひゃく
7	なな、しち	800	はっぴゃく
8	はち	900	きゅうひゃく
9	きゅう、く		
10	じゅう	1,000	せん
11	じゅういち	2,000	にせん
12	じゅうに	3,000	さんぜん
13	じゅうさん	4,000	よんせん
14	じゅうよん、じゅうし	5,000	ごせん
15	じゅうご	6,000	ろくせん
16	じゅうろく	7,000	ななせん
17	じゅうなな、じゅうしち	8,000	はっせん
18	じゅうはち	9,000	きゅうせん
19	じゅうきゅう、じゅうく		
20	にじゅう	10,000	いちまん
30	さんじゅう	100,000	じゅうまん
40	よんじゅう	1,000,000	ひゃくまん
50	ごじゅう	10,000,000	せんまん
60	ろくじゅう	100,000,000	いちおく
70	ななじゅう、しちじゅう		
80	はちじゅう	17.5	じゅうななてんご
90	きゅうじゅう	0.83	れいてんはちさん

$$\frac{1}{2} \quad にぶんの いち$$

$$\frac{3}{4} \quad よんぶんの さん$$

II . Expressions of time

day	morning	night
おととい the day before yesterday	おとといの あさ the morning before last	おとといの ばん(よる) the night before last
きのう yesterday	きのうの あさ yesterday morning	きのうの ばん(よる) last night
きょう today	けさ this morning	こんばん(きょうの よる) tonight
あした tomorrow	あしたの あさ tomorrow morning	あしたの ばん(よる) tomorrow night
あさって the day after tomorrow	あさっての あさ the morning after next	あさっての ばん(よる) the night after next
まいにち every day	まいあさ every morning	まいばん every night

week	month	year
せんせんしゅう (にしゅうかんまえ) the week before last	せんせんげつ (にかげつまえ) the month before last	おととし the year before last
せんしゅう last week	せんげつ last month	きょねん last year
こんしゅう this week	こんげつ this month	ことし this year
らいしゅう next week	らいげつ next month	らいねん next year
さらいしゅう the week after next	さらいげつ the month after next	さらいねん the year after next
まいしゅう every week	まいつき every month	まいとし、まいねん every year

Telling time

o'clock 一時		minute 一分	
1	いちじ	1	いっぷん
2	にじ	2	にふん
3	さんじ	3	さんぷん
4	よじ	4	よんぷん
5	ごじ	5	ごふん
6	ろくじ	6	ろっぷん
7	しちじ	7	ななふん
8	はちじ	8	はっぷん
9	くじ	9	きゅうふん
10	じゅうじ	10	じゅっぷん、じっぷん
11	じゅういちじ	15	じゅうごふん
12	じゅうにじ	30	さんじゅっぷん、さんじっぷん、はん
?	なんじ	?	なんぷん

the days of the week ～曜日	
にちようび	Sunday
げつようび	Monday
かようび	Tuesday
すいようび	Wednesday
もくようび	Thursday
きんようび	Friday
どようび	Saturday
なんようび	what day

date					
month 一月		day 一日			
1	いちがつ	1	ついたち	17	じゅうしちにち
2	にがつ	2	ふつか	18	じゅうはちにち
3	さんがつ	3	みっか	19	じゅうくにち
4	しがつ	4	よっか	20	はつか
5	ごがつ	5	いつか	21	にじゅういちにち
6	ろくがつ	6	むいか	22	にじゅうににち
7	しちがつ	7	なのか	23	にじゅうさんにち
8	はちがつ	8	ようか	24	にじゅうよっか
9	くがつ	9	ここのか	25	にじゅうごにち
10	じゅうがつ	10	とおか	26	にじゅうろくにち
11	じゅういちがつ	11	じゅういちにち	27	にじゅうしちにち
12	じゅうにがつ	12	じゅうににち	28	にじゅうはちにち
?	なんがつ	13	じゅうさんにち	29	にじゅうくにち
		14	じゅうよっか	30	さんじゅうにち
		15	じゅうごにち	31	さんじゅういちにち
		16	じゅうろくにち	?	なんにち

III. Expressions of period

time duration		
	hour 一時間	**minute** 一分
1	いちじかん	いっぷん
2	にじかん	にふん
3	さんじかん	さんぷん
4	よじかん	よんぷん
5	ごじかん	ごふん
6	ろくじかん	ろっぷん
7	ななじかん、しちじかん	ななふん
8	はちじかん	はっぷん
9	くじかん	きゅうふん
10	じゅうじかん	じゅっぷん、じっぷん
?	なんじかん	なんぷん

period			
	day 一日	**week** 一週間	**month** 一か月	**year** 一年
1	いちにち	いっしゅうかん	いっかげつ	いちねん
2	ふつか	にしゅうかん	にかげつ	にねん
3	みっか	さんしゅうかん	さんかげつ	さんねん
4	よっか	よんしゅうかん	よんかげつ	よねん
5	いつか	ごしゅうかん	ごかげつ	ごねん
6	むいか	ろくしゅうかん	ろっかげつ、はんとし	ろくねん
7	なのか	ななしゅうかん	ななかげつ	ななねん、しちねん
8	ようか	はっしゅうかん	はちかげつ、はっかげつ	はちねん
9	ここのか	きゅうしゅうかん	きゅうかげつ	きゅうねん
10	とおか	じゅっしゅうかん、じっしゅうかん	じゅっかげつ、じっかげつ	じゅうねん
?	なんにち	なんしゅうかん	なんかげつ	なんねん

IV. Counter suffixes

	things	persons	order	thin and flat things
		一人	一番	一枚
1	ひとつ	ひとり	いちばん	いちまい
2	ふたつ	ふたり	にばん	にまい
3	みっつ	さんにん	さんばん	さんまい
4	よっつ	よにん	よんばん	よんまい
5	いつつ	ごにん	ごばん	ごまい
6	むっつ	ろくにん	ろくばん	ろくまい
7	ななつ	ななにん、しちにん	ななばん	ななまい
8	やっつ	はちにん	はちばん	はちまい
9	ここのつ	きゅうにん	きゅうばん	きゅうまい
10	とお	じゅうにん	じゅうばん	じゅうまい
?	いくつ	なんにん	なんばん	なんまい

	machines and vehicles	age	books and notebooks	clothes
	一台	一歳	一冊	一着
1	いちだい	いっさい	いっさつ	いっちゃく
2	にだい	にさい	にさつ	にちゃく
3	さんだい	さんさい	さんさつ	さんちゃく
4	よんだい	よんさい	よんさつ	よんちゃく
5	ごだい	ごさい	ごさつ	ごちゃく
6	ろくだい	ろくさい	ろくさつ	ろくちゃく
7	ななだい	ななさい	ななさつ	ななちゃく
8	はちだい	はっさい	はっさつ	はっちゃく
9	きゅうだい	きゅうさい	きゅうさつ	きゅうちゃく
10	じゅうだい	じゅっさい、じっさい	じゅっさつ、じっさつ	じゅっちゃく、じっちゃく
?	なんだい	なんさい	なんさつ	なんちゃく

	frequency	small things	shoes and socks	houses
	一回	一個	一足	一軒
1	いっかい	いっこ	いっそく	いっけん
2	にかい	にこ	にそく	にけん
3	さんかい	さんこ	さんぞく	さんげん
4	よんかい	よんこ	よんそく	よんけん
5	ごかい	ごこ	ごそく	ごけん
6	ろっかい	ろっこ	ろくそく	ろっけん
7	ななかい	ななこ	ななそく	ななけん
8	はっかい	はっこ	はっそく	はっけん
9	きゅうかい	きゅうこ	きゅうそく	きゅうけん
10	じゅっかい、じっかい	じゅっこ、じっこ	じゅっそく、じっそく	じゅっけん、じっけん
?	なんかい	なんこ	なんぞく	なんげん

	floors of a building	thin and long things	drinks, etc., in cups and glasses	small animals, fish and insects
	一階	一本	一杯	一匹
1	いっかい	いっぽん	いっぱい	いっぴき
2	にかい	にほん	にはい	にひき
3	さんがい	さんぼん	さんばい	さんびき
4	よんかい	よんほん	よんはい	よんひき
5	ごかい	ごほん	ごはい	ごひき
6	ろっかい	ろっぽん	ろっぱい	ろっぴき
7	ななかい	ななほん	ななはい	ななひき
8	はっかい	はっぽん	はっぱい	はっぴき
9	きゅうかい	きゅうほん	きゅうはい	きゅうひき
10	じゅっかい、じっかい	じゅっぽん、じっぽん	じゅっぱい、じっぱい	じゅっぴき、じっぴき
?	なんがい	なんぼん	なんばい	なんびき

Ⅴ．Conjugations of verbs

Ⅰ－group

	ます-form		て-form	dictionary form
会います[ともだちに～]	あい	ます	あって	あう
遊びます	あそび	ます	あそんで	あそぶ
洗います	あらい	ます	あらって	あらう
あります	あり	ます	あって	ある
あります	あり	ます	あって	ある
あります[おまつりが～]	あり	ます	あって	ある
歩きます	あるき	ます	あるいて	あるく
言います	いい	ます	いって	いう
行きます	いき	ます	いって	いく
急ぎます	いそぎ	ます	いそいで	いそぐ
要ります[ビザが～]	いり	ます	いって	いる
動きます	うごき	ます	うごいて	うごく
歌います	うたい	ます	うたって	うたう
売ります	うり	ます	うって	うる
置きます	おき	ます	おいて	おく
送ります	おくり	ます	おくって	おくる
送ります[ひとを～]	おくり	ます	おくって	おくる
押します	おし	ます	おして	おす
思い出します	おもいだし	ます	おもいだして	おもいだす
思います	おもい	ます	おもって	おもう
泳ぎます	およぎ	ます	およいで	およぐ
下ろします[おかねを～]	おろし	ます	おろして	おろす
終わります	おわり	ます	おわって	おわる
買います	かい	ます	かって	かう
返します	かえし	ます	かえして	かえす
帰ります	かえり	ます	かえって	かえる
かかります	かかり	ます	かかって	かかる
書きます(かきます)	かき	ます	かいて	かく
貸します	かし	ます	かして	かす
勝ちます	かち	ます	かって	かつ
かぶります	かぶり	ます	かぶって	かぶる
頑張ります	がんばり	ます	がんばって	がんばる

ない-form		た-form	meaning	lesson
あわ	ない	あった	meet [a friend]	6
あそば	ない	あそんだ	enjoy oneself, play	13
あらわ	ない	あらった	wash	18
―	ない	あった	have	9
―	ない	あった	exist, be (referring to inanimate things)	10
―	ない	あった	[a festival] be held, take place	21
あるか	ない	あるいた	walk	23
いわ	ない	いった	say	21
いか	ない	いった	go	5
いそが	ない	いそいだ	hurry	14
いら	ない	いった	need, require [a visa]	20
うごか	ない	うごいた	move, work	21
うたわ	ない	うたった	sing	18
うら	ない	うった	sell	15
おか	ない	おいた	put	15
おくら	ない	おくった	send	7
おくら	ない	おくった	escort [someone], go with	24
おさ	ない	おした	push, press	16
おもいださ	ない	おもいだした	remember, recollect	15
おもわ	ない	おもった	think	21
およが	ない	およいだ	swim	13
おろさ	ない	おろした	withdraw	16
おわら	ない	おわった	finish	4
かわ	ない	かった	buy	6
かえさ	ない	かえした	give back, return	17
かえら	ない	かえった	go home, return	5
かから	ない	かかった	take, cost (referring to time or money)	11
かか	ない	かいた	write, draw, paint	6
かさ	ない	かした	lend	7
かた	ない	かった	win	21
かぶら	ない	かぶった	put on (a hat, etc.)	22
がんばら	ない	がんばった	do one's best	25

	ます-form		て-form	dictionary form
聞きます	きき	ます	きいて	きく
聞きます[せんせいに ～]	きき	ます	きいて	きく
切ります	きり	ます	きって	きる
消します	けし	ます	けして	けす
触ります[ドアに ～]	さわり	ます	さわって	さわる
知ります	しり	ます	しって	しる
吸います[たばこを ～]	すい	ます	すって	すう
住みます	すみ	ます	すんで	すむ
座ります	すわり	ます	すわって	すわる
出します	だし	ます	だして	だす
立ちます	たち	ます	たって	たつ
使います	つかい	ます	つかって	つかう
着きます	つき	ます	ついて	つく
作ります、造ります	つくり	ます	つくって	つくる
連れて 行きます	つれて いき	ます	つれて いって	つれて いく
手伝います	てつだい	ます	てつだって	てつだう
泊まります[ホテルに ～]	とまり	ます	とまって	とまる
取ります	とり	ます	とって	とる
撮ります[しゃしんを ～]	とり	ます	とって	とる
取ります[としを ～]	とり	ます	とって	とる
直します	なおし	ます	なおして	なおす
なくします	なくし	ます	なくして	なくす
習います	ならい	ます	ならって	ならう
なります	なり	ます	なって	なる
脱ぎます	ぬぎ	ます	ぬいで	ぬぐ
登ります、上ります	のぼり	ます	のぼって	のぼる
飲みます	のみ	ます	のんで	のむ
飲みます	のみ	ます	のんで	のむ
飲みます[くすりを ～]	のみ	ます	のんで	のむ
乗ります[でんしゃに ～]	のり	ます	のって	のる
入ります[きっさてんに ～]	はいり	ます	はいって	はいる
入ります[だいがくに ～]	はいり	ます	はいって	はいる
入ります[おふろに ～]	はいり	ます	はいって	はいる
はきます	はき	ます	はいて	はく

ない-form		た-form	meaning	lesson
きか	ない	きいた	hear, listen	6
きか	ない	きいた	ask [the teacher]	23
きら	ない	きった	cut, slice	7
けさ	ない	けした	turn off	14
さわら	ない	さわった	touch [a door]	23
しら	ない	しった	get to know	15
すわ	ない	すった	smoke [a cigarette]	6
すま	ない	すんだ	be going to live	15
すわら	ない	すわった	sit down	14
ださ	ない	だした	take out, hand in, send	16
たた	ない	たった	stand up	14
つかわ	ない	つかった	use	14
つか	ない	ついた	arrive	25
つくら	ない	つくった	make, produce	15
つれて いか	ない	つれて いった	take (someone)	24
てつだわ	ない	てつだった	help (with a task)	14
とまら	ない	とまった	stay [at a hotel]	19
とら	ない	とった	take, pass	14
とら	ない	とった	take [a photograph]	6
とら	ない	とった	grow old	25
なおさ	ない	なおした	repair, correct	24
なくさ	ない	なくした	lose	17
ならわ	ない	ならった	learn	7
なら	ない	なった	become	19
ぬが	ない	ぬいだ	take off (clothes, shoes, etc.)	17
のぼら	ない	のぼった	climb, go up	19
のま	ない	のんだ	drink	6
のま	ない	のんだ	drink alcohol	16
のま	ない	のんだ	take [medicine]	17
のら	ない	のった	ride, get on [a train]	16
はいら	ない	はいった	enter [a café]	14
はいら	ない	はいった	enter [university]	16
はいら	ない	はいった	take [a bath]	17
はか	ない	はいた	put on (shoes, trousers, etc.)	22

	ます-form		て-form	dictionary form
働きます	はたらき	ます	はたらいて	はたらく
話します	はなし	ます	はなして	はなす
払います	はらい	ます	はらって	はらう
弾きます	ひき	ます	ひいて	ひく
引きます	ひき	ます	ひいて	ひく
降ります[あめが 〜]	ふり	ます	ふって	ふる
曲がります[みぎへ 〜]	まがり	ます	まがって	まがる
待ちます	まち	ます	まって	まつ
回します	まわし	ます	まわして	まわす
持ちます	もち	ます	もって	もつ
持って 行きます	もって いき	ます	もって いって	もって いく
もらいます	もらい	ます	もらって	もらう
役に 立ちます	やくに たち	ます	やくに たって	やくに たつ
休みます	やすみ	ます	やすんで	やすむ
休みます[かいしゃを 〜]	やすみ	ます	やすんで	やすむ
呼びます	よび	ます	よんで	よぶ
読みます	よみ	ます	よんで	よむ
わかります	わかり	ます	わかって	わかる
渡ります[はしを 〜]	わたり	ます	わたって	わたる

ない-form		た-form	meaning	lesson
はたらか	ない	はたらいた	work	4
はなさ	ない	はなした	speak, talk	14
はらわ	ない	はらった	pay	17
ひか	ない	ひいた	play (stringed instrument, piano, etc.)	18
ひか	ない	ひいた	pull	23
ふら	ない	ふった	rain	14
まがら	ない	まがった	turn [to the right]	23
また	ない	まった	wait	14
まわさ	ない	まわした	turn	23
もた	ない	もった	hold	14
もって いか	ない	もって いった	take (something)	17
もらわ	ない	もらった	receive	7
やくに たた	ない	やくに たった	be useful	21
やすま	ない	やすんだ	take a rest, take a holiday	4
やすま	ない	やすんだ	take a day off [work]	11
よば	ない	よんだ	call	14
よま	ない	よんだ	read	6
わから	ない	わかった	understand	9
わたら	ない	わたった	cross [a bridge]	23

II − group

	ます -form		て -form	dictionary form
開けます	あけ	ます	あけて	あける
あげます	あげ	ます	あげて	あげる
集めます	あつめ	ます	あつめて	あつめる
浴びます[シャワーを 〜]	あび	ます	あびて	あびる
います	い	ます	いて	いる
います[こどもが 〜]	い	ます	いて	いる
います[にほんに 〜]	い	ます	いて	いる
入れます	いれ	ます	いれて	いれる
生まれます	うまれ	ます	うまれて	うまれる
起きます	おき	ます	おきて	おきる
教えます	おしえ	ます	おしえて	おしえる
教えます[じゅうしょを 〜]	おしえ	ます	おしえて	おしえる
覚えます	おぼえ	ます	おぼえて	おぼえる
降ります[でんしゃを 〜]	おり	ます	おりて	おりる
換えます	かえ	ます	かえて	かえる
変えます	かえ	ます	かえて	かえる
かけます[でんわを 〜]	かけ	ます	かけて	かける
かけます[めがねを 〜]	かけ	ます	かけて	かける
借ります	かり	ます	かりて	かりる
考えます	かんがえ	ます	かんがえて	かんがえる
着ます	き	ます	きて	きる
気を つけます	きを つけ	ます	きを つけて	きを つける
くれます	くれ	ます	くれて	くれる
閉めます	しめ	ます	しめて	しめる
調べます	しらべ	ます	しらべて	しらべる
捨てます	すて	ます	すてて	すてる
食べます	たべ	ます	たべて	たべる
足ります	たり	ます	たりて	たりる
疲れます	つかれ	ます	つかれて	つかれる
つけます	つけ	ます	つけて	つける
出かけます	でかけ	ます	でかけて	でかける
できます	でき	ます	できて	できる
出ます[おつりが 〜]	で	ます	でて	でる

ない -form		た -form	meaning	lesson
あけ	ない	あけた	open	14
あげ	ない	あげた	give	7
あつめ	ない	あつめた	collect, gather	18
あび	ない	あびた	take [a shower]	16
い	ない	いた	exist, be (referring to animate things)	10
い	ない	いた	have [a child]	11
い	ない	いた	stay, be [in Japan]	11
いれ	ない	いれた	put in, insert	16
うまれ	ない	うまれた	be born	22
おき	ない	おきた	get up, wake up	4
おしえ	ない	おしえた	teach	7
おしえ	ない	おしえた	tell [an address]	14
おぼえ	ない	おぼえた	memorise	17
おり	ない	おりた	get off [a train]	16
かえ	ない	かえた	exchange, change	18
かえ	ない	かえた	change	23
かけ	ない	かけた	make [a telephone call]	7
かけ	ない	かけた	put on [glasses]	22
かり	ない	かりた	borrow	7
かんがえ	ない	かんがえた	think, consider	25
き	ない	きた	put on (a shirt, etc.)	22
きを つけ	ない	きを つけた	pay attention, take care	21
くれ	ない	くれた	give (me)	24
しめ	ない	しめた	close, shut	14
しらべ	ない	しらべた	check, investigate	20
すて	ない	すてた	throw away	18
たべ	ない	たべた	eat	6
たり	ない	たりた	be enough, be sufficient	25
つかれ	ない	つかれた	get tired	13
つけ	ない	つけた	turn on	14
でかけ	ない	でかけた	go out	17
でき	ない	できた	be able to, can	18
で	ない	でた	[change] come out	23

	ます-form		て-form	dictionary form
出ます[きっさてんを～]	で	ます	でて	でる
出ます[だいがくを～]	で	ます	でて	でる
止めます	とめ	ます	とめて	とめる
寝ます	ね	ます	ねて	ねる
乗り換えます	のりかえ	ます	のりかえて	のりかえる
始めます	はじめ	ます	はじめて	はじめる
負けます	まけ	ます	まけて	まける
見せます	みせ	ます	みせて	みせる
見ます	み	ます	みて	みる
迎えます	むかえ	ます	むかえて	むかえる
やめます[かいしゃを～]	やめ	ます	やめて	やめる
忘れます	わすれ	ます	わすれて	わすれる

ない-form		た-form	meaning	lesson
で	ない	でた	go out [of a café]	14
で	ない	でた	graduate from [university]	16
とめ	ない	とめた	stop, park	14
ね	ない	ねた	sleep, go to bed	4
のりかえ	ない	のりかえた	change (train, etc.)	16
はじめ	ない	はじめた	start, begin	16
まけ	ない	まけた	lose, be beaten	21
みせ	ない	みせた	show	14
み	ない	みた	see, look at, watch	6
むかえ	ない	むかえた	go to meet, welcome	13
やめ	ない	やめた	quit or retire from [a company], stop, give up	21
わすれ	ない	わすれた	forget	17

III − group

	ます-form		て-form	dictionary form
案内します	あんないし	ます	あんないして	あんないする
運転します	うんてんし	ます	うんてんして	うんてんする
買い物します	かいものし	ます	かいものして	かいものする
来ます	き	ます	きて	くる
結婚します	けっこんし	ます	けっこんして	けっこんする
見学します	けんがくし	ます	けんがくして	けんがくする
研究します	けんきゅうし	ます	けんきゅうして	けんきゅうする
コピーします	コピーし	ます	コピーして	コピーする
散歩します[こうえんを〜]	さんぽし	ます	さんぽして	さんぽする
残業します	ざんぎょうし	ます	ざんぎょうして	ざんぎょうする
します	し	ます	して	する
します[ネクタイを〜]	し	ます	して	する
修理します	しゅうりし	ます	しゅうりして	しゅうりする
出張します	しゅっちょうし	ます	しゅっちょうして	しゅっちょうする
紹介します	しょうかいし	ます	しょうかいして	しょうかいする
食事します	しょくじし	ます	しょくじして	しょくじする
心配します	しんぱいし	ます	しんぱいして	しんぱいする
説明します	せつめいし	ます	せつめいして	せつめいする
洗濯します	せんたくし	ます	せんたくして	せんたくする
掃除します	そうじし	ます	そうじして	そうじする
連れて 来ます	つれて き	ます	つれて きて	つれて くる
電話します	でんわし	ます	でんわして	でんわする
勉強します	べんきょうし	ます	べんきょうして	べんきょうする
持って 来ます	もって き	ます	もって きて	もって くる
予約します	よやくし	ます	よやくして	よやくする
留学します	りゅうがくし	ます	りゅうがくして	りゅうがくする

ない-form		た-form	meaning	lesson
あんないし	ない	あんないした	show around, show the way	24
うんてんし	ない	うんてんした	drive	18
かいものし	ない	かいものした	do shopping	13
こ	ない	きた	come	5
けっこんし	ない	けっこんした	marry, get married	13
けんがくし	ない	けんがくした	tour, visit a place to study it	16
けんきゅうし	ない	けんきゅうした	do research	15
コピーし	ない	コピーした	copy	14
さんぽし	ない	さんぽした	take a walk [in a park]	13
ざんぎょうし	ない	ざんぎょうした	work overtime	17
し	ない	した	do, play	6
し	ない	した	put on [tie]	22
しゅうりし	ない	しゅうりした	repair	20
しゅっちょうし	ない	しゅっちょうした	go on a business trip	17
しょうかいし	ない	しょうかいした	introduce	24
しょくじし	ない	しょくじした	have a meal, dine	13
しんぱいし	ない	しんぱいした	worry	17
せつめいし	ない	せつめいした	explain	24
せんたくし	ない	せんたくした	wash (clothes)	19
そうじし	ない	そうじした	clean (a room)	19
つれて こ	ない	つれて きた	bring (someone)	24
でんわし	ない	でんわした	phone	16
べんきょうし	ない	べんきょうした	study	4
もって こ	ない	もって きた	bring (something)	17
よやくし	ない	よやくした	reserve, book	18
りゅうがくし	ない	りゅうがくした	study abroad	21

監修　Supervisor
鶴尾能子（Tsuruo Yoshiko）　石沢弘子（Ishizawa Hiroko）

執筆協力　Contributors
田中よね（Tanaka Yone）　澤田幸子（Sawada Sachiko）　重川明美（Shigekawa Akemi）
牧野昭子（Makino Akiko）　御子神慶子（Mikogami Keiko）

英語翻訳　English translator
John H. Loftus

本文イラスト　Illustrator
田辺澄美（Tanabe Kiyomi）　佐藤夏枝（Sato Natsue）

装丁・本文デザイン　Cover and Layout Designer
山田武（Yamada Takeshi）

写真提供
栃木県、姫路市、広島県

みんなの日本語　初級 I　第 2 版
翻訳・文法解説　英語版

1998年 3 月16日　初版第 1 刷発行
2012年 8 月 2 日　第 2 版第 1 刷発行
2014年10月24日　第 2 版第 4 刷発行

編著者　スリーエーネットワーク
発行者　藤嵜政子
発　行　株式会社スリーエーネットワーク
〒102-0083　東京都千代田区麹町 3 丁目 4 番
トラスティ麹町ビル 2 F
電話　営業　03（5275）2722
編集　03（5275）2725
http://www.3anet.co.jp/
印　刷　倉敷印刷株式会社

ISBN978-4-88319-604-3 C0081

みんなの日本語シリーズ

スリーエーネットワーク　　ホームページで新刊や日本語セミナーをご案内しております。
http://www.3anet.co.jp/